Criminal Justice
Recent Scholarship

Edited by
Marilyn McShane and Frank P. Williams III

A Series from LFB Scholarly

Table of Contents

List of Tables

List of Figures

Chapter 1
Introduction

Introduction and Research Problem

Since the bombings on September 11, 2001, interest and academic research in both international and transnational crime has been increasing (see Bennett, 2004). Indeed, more recent occurrences of transnational criminal activity and the capture or killing of high-level terrorists has resulted in research that has sought out better understandings of crime in different countries and how crime has become increasingly transnational in nature. To a lesser extent, studies have also examined and compared the structure and operation of institutions in different criminal justice systems and how those operations and policies may differ on the world stage (see for example Bayley, 1985; Waddington, 1999; see also Bennett, 2004; Olsen et al., 2010). Even fewer studies have examined extra-legal factors that may influence police officers' (or other criminal justice workers') discretionary responses. The purpose of this study is to shed light on what police officers believe to be disrespectful citizen behaviors and to compare the factors that influence how often officers experience disrespect from citizens in two first-world countries.

In the United States, numerous studies have been conducted which have examined the effects of extra-legal variables on police decision-making. Within that realm, studies have focused on the influence of a suspect's antagonistic demeanor and disrespect toward the police on the decision to arrest or use force. Many have found that the severity of outcome in a low level encounter may very well be in the hands (and mouth) of the suspect. The research has all but definitively concluded that when a suspect displays an antagonistic demeanor, is disrespectful, hostile, or fails to defer to the officer's authority, the probability that the officer will arrest or use force on that suspect increases (Piliavin and Briar, 1964; Black and Reiss, 1970; Freidrich, 1980; Worden, 1989; Lundman, 1994, 1996; Mastrofski et al., 1995; Worden and Shepard, 1996; Engel et al., 2000; Novak and Engel, 2005; Terrill and Paoline, 2007).

While scholars have generally agreed that antagonistic behavior is an important situational predictor of police behavior, the research reflects little agreement with the behaviors that constitute disrespect. Previous research has defined disrespect in a variety of ways, with little or no clear association between the concept and the indicators used (see Worden and Shepard, 1996), and it has been suggested that behaviors which officers deem to be disrespectful may not be adequately captured by any one study (Worden et al., 1996). In fact, no two studies have defined disrespect in the same manner. Instead, most conceptualizations utilize a variety of measures focused on citizen deference, civility, or cooperation. This may be partially due to the fact that observational studies have relied on researcher-driven conceptualizations rather than having sought to understand what officers themselves believe to be disrespectful. In doing so, these conceptualizations may be limited by the reliance on observers to interpret and properly code a citizen's behavior and the officer's response to that behavior. In short, research in the U.S. may not adequately capture the meaningful cues that signify disrespect in officers' eyes and given this, the definitional inconsistencies make it problematic to assess the body of literature as a whole.

These findings are limited to police in the U.S. because over the past 50 years, most of the extant research in this area has come out of the U.S. In fact, very little research has been conducted on the effect of disrespect in the past decade. Comparative research has been increasing but much of that research has focused on the socio-cultural aspects of crime, differences in crime and crime rates, and how crime has become increasingly transnational in nature (see for example Gertz and Myers, 1992; Marenin, 1997; Bennett, 2004; Olsen et al., 2010). Studies also have examined police operations and structure (see for example Bayley, 1985; Bennett, 2004; Gibbs et al., 2010) but a significant gap in the literature exists in that research in other countries has largely ignored the impact of extra-legal citizen behaviors on the use or abuse of discretion.

The United Kingdom is no exception and research examining extralegal factors that influence police decision-making is not extensive. In fact, no study there has examined the effect of disrespect or antagonistic demeanor on outcomes in police-citizen encounters. Waddington (2008) stated that the lack of research in this area stemmed from the fact that use of force by police is rare and without baseline evidence regarding uses of force, "we are unable to identify what, if anything, distinguishes circumstances leading to adverse outcomes from those that do not" (2008: 486). More generally, Neyroud (2009) suggested that while useful, policing research is seen as non-essential and is not valued in policing in the U.K. (see also Jackson and Bradford, 2009). As a result of this relatively unexplored area of research, it is unknown how often officers in the U.K. perceive that citizens are acting disrespectfully and whether differences exist between police officers in the U.K. and their counterparts in the U.S.

Moreover, no study has been conducted in either country that addresses the prevalence of perceived disrespectful behaviors in general, perceived disrespect in specific types of police-citizen encounters, or the factors that may lead to those perceptions. As such, this research adds to the current state of comparative police research by comparing officers' perceptions of (disrespectful) citizen behavior in police-citizen encounters instead of examining differences related to crime, crime rates, and organization structure. The possibility exists that police subculture varies from organization to organization and from country to country and that some of the variation stems from officer differences (Westmarland, 2008). As such, this study also compares characteristics of officers in an effort to determine if they influence how often officers experience disrespect. These factors include levels of productivity and cynicism, officer demographics, and current patrol assignment.

In sum, it is unknown how factors related to officers, their role/function, or police subculture influence the amount of disrespect that is directed toward them. It is important in its own right to examine the influence of these factors on experiencing disrespect in each individual country but as outlined in the contributions section below, it is as important to be able to compare officers in both countries to see if differences exist and to ascertain what influences those differences. The purpose of this research is to fill these gaps.

Purpose of the Study

In both countries, the research examining what police officers deem to be disrespectful is lacking. In the U.S., researcher-driven definitions have been inconsistent and at times, incomplete. Even as most causal research finds that disrespect influences police discretion, it is difficult to know if individual studies are measuring the same thing. In the U.K., the same cannot be said since no empirical study has been undertaken involving citizen disrespect and police decision-making. This study seeks to add to the body of literature by examining and comparing officers' perceptions and experiences of disrespect. It must be noted that this study seeks to understand the behaviors that officers associate with disrespect but does not seek to determine if those disrespectful behaviors influence officers' outcome decisions.

First, this research seeks to understand the breadth of behaviors that officer perceive to be disrespectful in both the United States and the United Kingdom. Stated differently, what are the behaviors which indicate to officers that citizens have stepped outside their preconceived subservient role? In the U.S., this can lead to operational definitions that can then be utilized for future observational studies and in the U.K., this research can serve as the starting point for studies examining the effect of disrespectful citizen behavior on police discretion. In both countries, the results can be utilized in police operations and training regimens.

The second goal is to examine officers' experiences with citizen disrespect in both countries and to compare those perceptions. The commonalities and perceptions will be cross-nationally compared with hypotheses related to general law enforcement-based factors, occupation-based factors, and officer-based factors. This research will also discover the prevalence of these behaviors both generally and in different types of encounters, and will uncover which behaviors officers find to be the most egregious ones.

Overview of the Data and Methods

Data for the analysis consists of information based on surveys distributed in two municipal police departments; The Oak Ridge Police Department (a pseudonym) in the southeastern U.S. and the London Metropolitan Police in the U.K. Oak Ridge has a population of approximately 250,000 and the City of Oak Ridge Police Department employs approximately 540 sworn personnel of which 400 are uniformed officers. For this study, only those officers on regular patrol were surveyed. London clearly has a much larger population than Oak Ridge (approximately 7.5 million) but like most larger municipal departments in the U.S. including Oak Ridge, they are structurally and functionally similar (this will be addressed further in Chapter 2). Virtually identical surveys were distributed in the spring of 2007.[1] A total of 450 surveys were distributed. In Oak Ridge, 200 surveys were distributed evenly over the city's four patrol sectors over a two-day period (March, 2007) with a total of 79 officers returning completed surveys. In London, 250 surveys were distributed over a three-day period (May 2007) with a total of 92 officers returning completed surveys. Only line patrol officers were included in this research and in both departments, surveys were given to all officers coming onto consecutive shifts until all of the surveys were distributed.

Both descriptive and explanatory analyses will be conducted. Included in the descriptive statistics will be frequencies in relation to the prevalence of disrespectful behaviors generally and how often specific types of disrespectful behaviors occur in specific types of police-citizen encounters. The analyses will include ordinary least squares regression, linear probability models, and logistic regressions conducted on variety scores of the dependent variables. Where appropriate, Poisson regressions will also be run as sensitivity tests to ensure that the results are robust.

Contribution to the Literature

At their foundation, police encounters are interactions between two or more people where the roles of each participant are known at the outset. If one of the goals of police research is to understand how and why officers act the way they do, then it is crucial to understand how they define interactions, and how they perceive and interpret the behaviors of citizens during these interactions. Past police research is limited in

---

[1] The only differences were changes to the sector/patrol area names, officer titles (police officer versus police constable), and offense names (i.e. driving under the influence versus drink drive). See Appendix I for the survey instrument distributed to Oak Ridge officers and Appendix II for the survey instrument distributed to London officers.

this respect in that studies have not asked officers directly how they perceive certain behaviors. Studies have attempted to determine how officers respond to situational cues but none have examined how officers interpret the citizen's action that leads to their response. With this in mind, the outcome of this research will advance the field in the following ways.

In relation to understanding how citizen disrespect influences police behavior, the evidence has relied solely on researcher-driven conceptualizations in observational studies. This does not imply that observational research is biased. In fact, the results from observational research have revealed more about police decision-making than studies utilizing other data collection methodologies. Other than one exploratory study, this will be the first research to ask officers how they see and perceive citizen disrespect and the results here will reveal the breadth of behaviors that make up disrespect in officers' eyes. So while systematic observation may be the most sensible methodology to examine police behaviors, it may not be as useful in determining how officers interpret citizens' behaviors. With this important new information in hand, future research, including observational research, can work toward a consistent conceptualization of disrespect based on a definition provided by officers rather than researchers. A conceptualization of this kind should lead to increased levels of validity and reliability and as these levels increase, a better understanding of police reactions will follow.

Second, the research will reveal which specific citizen behaviors occur more often in different types of encounters, regardless of whether or not officers find a specific behavior to be disrespectful. For example, a refusal to obey commands could be more prevalent in traffic stops that eventually lead to a criminal or DUI arrest than in traffic stops that only result in a citation. With the many discretionary choices available to officers in the different stages of any given encounter, this information can give officers the ability to modify their interpretation of the situation as that situation unfolds and to change their own behavior accordingly. This information could have significant implications for police training and role play training in specific, by giving rookie officers another investigative tool to use during different types of encounters.

In turn, if officers can be trained to be conscious of how disrespectful behaviors may affect them, then officers can begin to de-escalate a situation while avoiding any official or unofficial sanctioning of citizens that result directly from such behaviors. While maintaining control during any situation is crucial for officers in the field in any country, the hope exists that officers could be trained to base their discretionary decisions on legal justifications rather than extralegal ones and hence not react to disrespect when they encounter it. While understanding which citizen behaviors will be exhibited in certain interactions may be logical and intuitive, it is still important to garner empirical support for such assertions.

Third, save for the effect of race, no study in the U.K. has examined the effect of extra-legal characteristics on police decision making (see Delsol and Shiner, 2006). With a wide open field of study, this research can contribute by obtaining an understanding of what British officers believe to be disrespectful behavior, and how often they experience it generally and in specific types of encounters. Moreover, this can be the starting point for future research that seeks to determine if citizen disrespect influences officers' decisions to ticket, arrest, or use physical force.

Fourth, by cross-nationally comparing officers' experiences with disrespect, a better understanding of how similar and different police are will result. The more that is known about how separate criminal justice systems operate, the better prepared we are to identify trends that transcend borders. If the research finds that experiences with disrespect are alike, it will support the notion that police in the U.S. and England are more similar than not. If the research does find differences, then police in both countries can begin to understand what department or officer-based factors contribute to such experiences. This knowledge can then be utilized as a guide for future explanatory research as well as in police training. Currently, comparative research has had little impact on policy making, especially in relation to policing in the U.S. Comparatively examining the impact of department and officer-based variables instead of citizen or environmental-based variables allows for change to begin from within departments rather than relying on citizens to change.

Fifth, most comparative studies focus on measuring crime and crime rates. These types of transnational studies suffer due to differing definitions of crime, specificity levels of crime measurement, and amounts of information actually revealed by the countries being studied. The cross-national comparisons in this study will avoid these issues since officers in both English speaking countries answered questions on virtually identical survey instruments. It will also provide valuable insight into understanding the similarities and differences of officers' perceptions of citizen behavior in both countries.

Limitations

Factors exist that present limitations for this study. These will be outlined in more detail in the relevant chapters and in the discussion chapter but a brief introduction to the limitations is warranted here. First, the sample for this research is relatively small (171 total officers in the sample; 79 in Oak Ridge and 92 in London) and the response rates were low for both departments. This limits what can be accomplished statistically and limits the generalizability of the research. The sample was also gained through non-probabilistic methods. Purposive sampling was utilized and without the benefit of a truly random sample, the possibility exists that the results of the analyses may not reveal a true reflection of the departments in the sample.

Second, practical limitations are also present. It must be acknowledged that the sample includes two departments with notable organizational strength differences. Oak Ridge employs approximately 540 uniformed officers while the London Metropolitan Police (MET) employs over 30,000. Additionally, the MET is the largest police department in the U.K. and as such, may not be representative of all departments in the U.K.

In whole, it must be acknowledged that both methodological and practical limitations exist in this research and they must be taken into consideration. Even with these limitations, there are clear needs for answers to questions have gone unanswered. Do officers from different countries experience similar behaviors from citizens? Are there characteristics of a country's culture that influence the probability of experiencing disrespectful behavior or even influence how officers define disrespect? By comparing these perceptions and experiences, police in each country may gain a better understanding into the dynamics of interactions, how they can change based on a perception of disrespect, and the role that cultural and officers' differences play in those experiences.

Chapter 2
Disrespect and Police Outcomes in Two Countries

Introduction and Overview

In the U.S. and the U.K., the police exist to provide a service to the population. Whether engaging in crime prevention or detection, answering non-law enforcement related calls, or engaging in community policing activities, the police are present to exert a level of social control over the public that they deal with. The police are separate from citizens and are a powerful group with a mandate to coerce compliance when the situation dictates. With that power and authority comes an expectation that citizens (and anyone else present) will acquiesce and allow officers to control encounters that they are in.

Officers command and compel citizens to obey orders and comply with requests for information. More generally but equally important, citizens must immediately recognize the role that police play and must defer accordingly. When citizens fail to show deference, officers can use the wide discretion they have been given to re-assert their authority. This re-assertion could simply be a command to the citizen to cease their behavior but could also, dependent on the citizen's specific behavior, result in more formal sanctions, such as arrest or use of physical force. As Chevigny (1969:92) aptly stated: "Any challenge to a policeman...even if the challenge is legally justified, will be considered a dangerous threat to his authority."

Following Chevigny (see also Westley, 1959), the past four decades have seen a great deal of research in the U.S. which has examined discretionary decisions made by officers. Studies have investigated the legal and extra-legal factors that influence arrest and use of force and within this realm, the research has all but concluded that citizen disrespect influences these decisions. Unfortunately, the same cannot be said of policing research in the U.K. While there have been studies examining the police in the U.K., there has been a noticeable lack of research on the formal and informal factors that influence police decisions (see Reiner, 1992; Newburn, 2008; Neyroud, 2009). When attempting to examine the processual aspects of interactions, there is an ongoing action-reaction-action process. Relevant to this study, the citizen behaves in a specific manner (disrespectful), the officer observes the behavior and perceives it as disrespectful, and the officer then reacts to the disrespectful behavior. The current body of literature almost exclusively focuses on the first and third step by determining the causal factors that lead to an officer's reaction to a citizen's disrespectful behavior. In fact, no study has examined the factors that influence the perception of disrespect on the part of police.

With this in mind, the extant research reviewed below will address the research in each country individually and will be organized in the following fashion. The first major section will focus on the research in the U.S. and will chronologically differentiate between the early studies which blended conceptualizations of antagonistic demeanor and disrespect, and more recent research that has worked to separate the two for study. The importance of controlling for crime in causal research will then be addressed followed by limitations of the current body of research in the U.S.

The second section focuses on research, or more appropriately, the lack of research in the U.K. Very few studies have examined police discretionary decision-making but surprisingly, none have examined the influence of disrespect. In this section, the nature of police-citizen encounters will be addressed followed by the research examining the factors that influence police decision-making. The limitations of research in the U.K. will be examined followed by a chapter summary.

Police in the United States

Introduction

The discretionary decision making that police engage in has long been a focus of empirical research. This focus is reasonable given the relative autonomy from the organization and the wide discretion police have while on the job (see Lipsky, 1980). Police officers come into work, leave the station in a patrol vehicle and other than calls for service, they choose what they want to do and how they want to do it. In particular encounters, officers can choose from a variety of different options at contact, during the body of the encounter, and at exit (Bayley and Bittner, 1984) and specific choices made by an officer at any stage may influence the choices made at later stages. Certainly the substantive laws limit their discretion but the freedom to choose whom they want to stop, whom they want to ticket or arrest, and how to talk to citizens is largely up to them.

Westley (1959) was one of the first researchers to see this aspect of the job as problematic. He understood that with discretion came the possibility of abuses and that these abuses of discretion could be the result of citizens' behaviors unrelated to the original violation. After he found that police react negatively to disrespectful behaviors, a sizable body of literature followed that addressed and concurred with the contention that police punish citizens who are disrespectful or antagonistic toward them.

While the body of research is in general agreement, each study has used their own conceptualization of disrespect. Like use of physical force as a dependent variable, conceptualizations of disrespect have included a variety of behaviors. Some have included physical and gesture-based indicators while others limit their definition to strictly verbal indicators. In either case, it is important to understand the effect of disrespect on police behavior and how past research has conceptualized disrespect for study.

Early Studies - Antagonistic Demeanor and Disrespect as Explanatory Variables

In the early years of criminal justice research, there was a great deal of attention paid to the administration of criminal justice. In relation to policing, many of those works focused on how and why police officers acted and reacted in encounters with citizens. Despite the fact that the strong majority of police encounters are polite and lack any behavioral indications of citizen disrespect (see Sykes and Brent, 1983; and more recently, Dunham and Alpert, 2009), studies have found that police discretionary decisions were influenced by the behaviors of citizens and not just the particular violation of law. Specifically, research found that police will formally or informally punish citizens who act disrespectfully or display an antagonistic demeanor.

As Table 1 indicates, Westley (1959) was the first to assert that police sanction those whose behavior indicated disrespect for police authority. He found that police demanded respect and when a citizen was disrespectful (via a 'wise guy' attitude), officers believed that it was legitimate to use violence to coerce respect from them. Piliavin and Briar (1964) agreed, finding that juveniles who were cooperative were less likely to be arrested than uncooperative ones. They found that "youthful offenders who were fractious, obdurate, or who appeared nonchalant in their encounters with patrolmen were likely to be viewed as 'tough guys' or 'punks' who fully deserved the most severe sanction: arrest" (1964: 210). This conceptualization was more closely related to how the officers perceived and interpreted the more subtle behaviors rather than ones that were explicitly disrespectful toward them.

Black and Reiss (1967) indicated that police officers hold the authority position in any encounter and that they are more likely to respond punitively when citizens are hostile or antagonistic compared to citizens who show more deference or respect. Consistent with these assertions, Toch (1969) found that most encounters where force was used resulted from a citizen who showed disrespect to the officer, usually in the form of failing to abide by an officer's request or command. Both Reiss (1968) and Chevigny (1969) also found that force was more likely when citizens defied police or challenged their authority. Chevigny went on to state that "many incidents of the use of force by policemen bear an unfortunate resemblance to assaults by private citizens; they are hotheaded reactions to a real or imagined insult" (1969: 73).

Findings in these early studies led to increased attention on citizens' behaviors and how they influenced responses from officers. Following in the tradition of Westley and Chevigny, van Maanen (1978) described how officers who perceive disrespect from citizens label those citizens as 'assholes' and that when they do perceive disrespect, they deem it to be an occupational 'affront' and respond more punitively. Additionally, Brown (1981) described disrespect in terms of defiance and stated that when a citizen defied an officer's authority, that behavior was akin to the citizen flunking 'the attitude test.' Sykes and Brent (1983) agreed, stating that while most police encounters are cordial, if a citizen chooses not to defer to the officer's questions or commands, they can expect an authoritative or aggressive response almost immediately (see also Herbert, 2006).

Table 1. Conceptualizations of Disrespect and Outcomes in Early Studies

Study	Label	Conceptualization	Outcome
Westley, 1959	Disrespect for police authority	Wise guy attitude and impoliteness	Officers used violence to coerce respect from wise guys
Piliavin and Briar, 1964	Uncooperative	Cooperative or uncooperative demeanor	Uncooperative demeanor increased probability of arrest
Black and Reiss, 1967	Disrespect	Hostile, antagonistic, less deference, less respect	Disrespect led to punitive response by officer
Reiss, 1968	Disrespectful demeanor	Citizen challenged officer's authority via open defiance or refusal to obey commands	Disrespectful demeanor increased probability of physical force
Toch, 1969	Disrespect	Failing to abide by officer's command	Disrespect increased probability of physical force
Chevigny, 1969	Defiance of police authority	Citizen defied police or challenged their authority	Defiance increased likelihood of physical force

Table 1. (Continued) Conceptualizations of Disrespect and
Outcomes in Early Studies

Study	Label	Conceptualization	Outcome
Van Maanen, 1978	Perceived disrespect	Assholes - an occupational affront	Officers responded more punitively when they perceived disrespect
Friedrich, 1980	Demeanor	Antagonism	Antagonism increased probability of physical force
Brown, 1981	Disrespectful demeanor	Defiance of authority - flunked the attitude test	Disrespectful demeanor increased likelihood of formal police action
Sykes and Brent, 1983	Deference	Uncivil, uncooperative, Resisting	Non-deference increased likelihood of confrontation by officer

The importance of these early works lies in the fact that these authors did not limit themselves by stating that officers responded to only instantly recognizable acts of aggression. Instead, these works examined the more subtle forms of disrespect *and* perceived disrespect, and how they might influence an officer's behavior. Some of these early works also examined the influence of respect and deference separate from antagonistic behavior and even when labeled as 'disrespectful demeanor,' disrespect came with its own set of conceptualizations and measurements. This is exemplified by Reiss (1968) who discussed disrespect in relation to refusal to obey commands without equating these behaviors with hostile or antagonistic ones (see also Toch, 1969).

A clear pattern emerged from the early research. While these studies examined subtle forms of perceived disrespect, each study labeled and defined disrespect differently. Like 'use of physical force' as a dependent variable, disrespect as an independent variable was conceptualized in these early studies utilizing diverse labels and definitions (see for example Piliavin and Briar, 1964; Reiss, 1968; Brown, 1981). Rather than being detrimental, however, these differences advanced knowledge by demonstrating that disrespect could and did encompass many distinct behaviors and that those behaviors were not necessarily or overtly antagonistic (i.e. failing to abide by an officer's request). Moreover, the studies also showed that even with various conceptualizations, citizen disrespect consistently led to a punitive response from officers.

Since the late 1950's, research has continued to examine the effects that extra-legal variables have on police decision-making. While these early studies were the first to support the assertion that extra-legal factors such as disrespect did influence officers' decisions, they were not in agreement as to how disrespect should be conceptualized and how to disentangle disrespectful behaviors from antagonistic ones. This trend has been persistent. Even though recent studies have worked to separate disrespect from antagonistic demeanor, many have conceptualized disrespect in their own fashion and have continued to include attributes associated with antagonistic behavior.

Recent Studies: Conceptualizations of Disrespect as an Explanatory Variable and the Influence of Disrespect on Police Decision Making

The research that has been produced over the past two decades has shown that the explanatory power of disrespect on police decision-making may have decreased (see Terrill and Mastrofski, 2002). However, as Lundman (1996) and Worden et al. (1996) have suggested, the variation and decrease may be a product of how disrespect is conceptualized and represented in these analyses (see also Worden and Shepard, 1996). Moreover, the decrease may also be a result of how studies are measuring use of force as a dependent variable.[2] In either case, it is clear that these different

---

[2] Use of physical force, like disrespect, has been defined differently by many studies. For example, some have included only physical behaviors (see

conceptualizations have contributed to different results in causal research (see also Dunham and Alpert, 2009).

Varying conceptualizations from more recent studies have included general impoliteness, overly hostile acts (acts that physically threaten the officer), resistance (acts which challenge the officer's authority), and passive acts of noncompliance (failing to abide by the officer's requests) (see Worden et al.,1996). For example, Lundman's (1994) conceptualization differentiated between deferent statements, impolite statements (a single impolite statement and a greater than average number of impolite statements) and included a mixed category (where suspect was both deferent and polite in the same encounter). Terrill and Mastrofski's (2002) conceptualization excluded when a citizen denies commands, whereas the bulk of the existing literature included it as a measure of disrespect. Reisig et al. (2004) defined disrespect as either passive (ignoring officer's commands) or active (name calling, derogatory statements, slurs, and insulting gestures) while excluding any physical acts (flee, resist, hide, or impede the officer's intent). More recently, Dai et al. (2011) conceptualized disrespect as a dependent variable by including behaviors that were passive aggressive (citizen verbally complied but body language hinted that citizen was upset), moderately hostile (citizen verbally expressed that they were upset with officer), and highly hostile (blatant disrespect, swearing, personal insults toward officer). While this conceptualization focused on levels of hostility, it also excluded any physical acts.

When conceptualizing citizens' behaviors that are antagonistic yet short of physically aggressive, many studies utilized 'hostile or antagonistic demeanor' as their independent variable. These studies began to include disrespect in their definitions of antagonistic demeanor or labeled such behaviors as 'disrespectful demeanor' (Klinger, 1994; see also Worden, et al., 1996). Demeanor as a concept represents the way one behaves or conducts themselves and how they relate to another person in an exchange, and given this, a person's

---

Worden, 1995) while others have included verbal commands (see Klinger, 1995). Terrill and Mastrofski (2002) went further to include voice commands, hand-cuffing, and pat downs in their definition. As more behaviors (verbal or physical) have been added into operationalizations of force, the research has found that the prevalence of such force increases.

demeanor could be characterized as: antagonistic, hostile, polite, threatening, civil, or even disrespectful (among others). Essentially, demeanor can potentially encompass all attributes of a person's behavior and while it is appropriate to include behavioral indicators of disrespect in a conceptualization of (antagonistic) demeanor, a problem arises when the primary explanatory variable is disrespect instead of demeanor. As exemplified by the early studies, a definition of disrespect should not necessarily be limited to those behaviors that are antagonistic or hostile and as an example, one could envision a situation where a citizen's behavior, such as passive noncompliance, might not be deemed antagonistic but could still be considered disrespectful.

In the 1990's, a group of studies focused their efforts on demeanor as a primary explanatory variable. As Table 2 indicates, these studies have used similar definitions of demeanor yet no two have utilized the same conceptualization or operationalization. Even though they focused on antagonistic demeanor instead of disrespect, these studies drew from the principles of the early studies and their conceptualizations ranging from impoliteness to extreme hostility. In short, they focused on citizen behaviors that were affronts to officers.[3] For example, Klinger (1994; see also Klinger, 1996) operationalized demeanor utilizing four categories: apologetic, deferential, somewhat demeaning, and openly hostile, and eventually collapsed these categories into measures of non-hostility, hostility, and extreme hostility. Based on this, Klinger's analysis of the Metro-Dade data revealed that arrest decisions were *not* influenced by demeanor once crime was controlled for although he did later find that 'extreme hostility' did increase the odds of arrest (1996).[4] In his study, Klinger struggled to sufficiently distinguish between disrespect and antagonistic

---

[3] Mastrofski et al. (1995) examined citizen resistance rather than antagonistic demeanor but still included attributes of demeanor found in other studies.

[4] Klinger measured criminality at two distinct stages: pre-intervention and interaction. The pre-intervention phase included criminal conduct which occurred before the officer and citizen were in direct contact and was scaled from no crime to major violent crime. The interaction phase measured only violence either between citizens or between the officer and citizen.

behavior. Although labeled as 'disrespectful demeanor,' he conceptualized it as antagonism, gave indications that he would measure it as deference or respect, and then measured with broad categories of hostility that forced observers to make subjective coding judgments of the citizens' behaviors.[5] For example, Klinger classified refusing to answer an officer's question as a lack of deference but when collapsing his measures, this fell under the 'hostile' category.

Table 2. Conceptualizations of Demeanor and Outcomes in Recent Research

Study	Label	Conceptualization	Outcome
Lundman, 1994	Demeanor	Verbal indicators of deference - deferent, impolite, mixed	Hostile demeanor or impolitenes s increased probability of arrest
Klinger, 1994	Demeanor	Legally permissible behavior of citizens during interactions with police officers that indicates the degree of deference or respect they extend to the involved police officers (apologetic, deferential, somewhat demeaning, and openly hostile) Klinger eventually collapsed these categories into measures of non-hostility, hostility, and extreme hostility	Arrest decisions were not influenced by demeanor

---

[5] Klinger's definition mainly focused on the spoken word and criminal attacks but he did add one gesture that observers were instructed to code (raising the middle finger). He also discussed a gambit of behaviors including refusing to answer officers' questions, being uncooperative, and showing a lack of deference.

Table 2. (Continued) Conceptualizations of Demeanor and Outcomes in Recent Research

Study	Label	Conceptualization	Outcome
Mastrofski et al., 1995	Resistance	Legal and illegal forms of active resistance prior to arrest including refusal to obey a command, acted threateningly, or offered physical resistance. Excluded forms of hostility	Resistance increased probability of arrest
Worden, 1995	Demeanor	Hostile and antagonistic, or detached	Hostile demeanor increased probability of proper and improper use of force
Klinger, 1996	Demeanor	Level of hostility - non-hostile, hostile, extreme hostility	Extreme hostility increased the odds of arrest
Worden and Shepard, 1996	Demeanor	Utilized several measures: 1. civility, noncompliance, and verbal resistance 2. sarcastic, disrespectful, hostile 3. cool, detached, couldn't care less	Hostile demeanor increased likelihood of arrest
Dunham and Alpert, 2009	Demeanor	Verbal comments, actions, or body language that were not threatening/illegal but could be interpreted as either positive, neutral, or negative by the police officer	Positive and negative changes in demeanor based on demeanor changes of other actor

Even with different operationalizations, most studies continued to find that a citizen's hostile or antagonistic demeanor increased the probability of arrest or use of force (see Lundman, 1994; Mastrofski et al., 1995; Worden, 1995; Terrill and Paoline 2007; but see Klinger, 1994; 1996). Although research utilizing antagonistic demeanor as a predictor of police sanction continues to be performed, research in the past eight years has seen an increased focus on disrespect as a distinct independent variable. While past causal research has incorporated disrespect into their conceptualizations of demeanor, the more recent research has specifically conceptualized disrespect as its own primary explanatory variable.

The conceptualizations put forth in these recent studies move beyond measuring hostility and civility and toward a more complete range of behaviors that officers might find offensive (see Table 3). For example, one would not generally characterize a passive act of noncompliance or spitting in an officer's presence (see Terrill and Mastrofski, 2002) to be an example of an 'antagonistic demeanor' but these actions could certainly be construed as disrespectful in officers' eyes. Similarly, citizens' behaviors exhibited prior to any verbal contact such as fleeing or engaging in a pursuit could be considered disrespectful toward the officer but could not, under current conceptualizations, be considered antagonistic.[6]

Using the observational data produced from the POPN study, Terrill and Mastrofski (2002) centered on behaviors that exemplified a lack of deference toward officers, more akin to disrespect than antagonism. They included a scaled resistance variable[7] and a conceptualization of disrespect that was more comprehensive than past studies which included both verbal and gesture based indicators of

---

[6] All of the past studies have limited their definition of disrespect (and antagonistic demeanor) to citizen behaviors occurring in face-to-face encounters with police officers. None have included pre-interaction measures.

[7] The categories of resistance included: none, passive, verbal, defensive, and active.

disrespect.[8] Like Reisig et al. (2004), Terrill and Mastrofski's operationalization of disrespect included derogatory statements, spitting, and obscene gestures while at the same time excluding both verbal and physical acts of defiance.[9]

Like Terrill and Mastrofski (2002), Dai et al. (2011) examined disrespect as part of the larger sequence of events in an encounter but rather than determine what effect disrespect had on outcomes, they worked to determine what led to the disrespectful behavior in the first place. They found that citizen disrespect increased when police were disrespectful to them but that it decreased when police were acting forcefully. They also found that disrespect was more likely when there were several officers on the scene, when the citizen was intoxicated, when the citizen was female, or was nonwhite (2011).

To date, all of the causal research has utilized researcher-driven conceptualizations of disrespect rather than officer-driven conceptualizations and no conceptualization is consistent with any other study. Terrence (2005) was the first to focus on officers' perceptions of disrespectful behavior. He asked officers how they would react if a juvenile was disrespectful toward them but did not intentionally conceptualize disrespect. Instead, he left it up to the officers to determine what disrespect actually entailed (2005). Based on this, officers stated that they would be more likely to arrest a disrespectful juvenile over one that was not disrespectful.

One exploratory study did attempt to formulate an officer-based definition of disrespect. Pizio (2005) interviewed officers from a mid-sized city police department in an effort to obtain an officer-driven definition of disrespect. In this research, officers specified a range of verbal, physical, and gestural disrespectful behaviors that was more

---

[8] Their definition included: Verbal: calling the officer names, making derogatory statements about the officer or his family, making disparaging or belittling remarks, and slurs. Gestural: 'flipping the bird,' obscene gestures, and spitting in the presence of the officer.

[9] Reisig et. al. (2004) - Behaviors included: passive behaviors (ignoring officer's commands) and active behaviors (name calling, derogatory statements, slurs, and insulting gestures). Excluded physical behaviors included: flee, resist, hide, or impede the officer's intent.

extensive than past conceptualizations and that did include behaviors that were illegal. Table 4 outlines the behaviors included in Pizio's officer-based definition of disrespect (2005).

Table 3. Conceptualizations of Disrespect and Outcomes in Recent Research

Study	Label	Conceptualization	Outcome
Terrill, 2001 Terrill and Mastrofski, 2002	Disrespect	Verbal: calling the officer names, making derogatory statements about the officer or his family, making disparaging or belittling remarks, and slurs. Gestural: 'flipping the bird,' obscene gestures, and spitting in the presence of the officer Conceptualization excluded verbal and physical acts of defiance (i.e. refusal to obey commands, fleeing, resisting arrests)	While resistance did increase the likelihood of police use of force, disrespect had no influence on use of force
Engel, 2003	Disrespect	Noncompliance, verbally resistant, physically resistant but how observers characterized disrespect was not known	Non-whites and females had increased probability of disrespect

Table 3. (Continued) Conceptualizations of Disrespect and Outcomes in Recent Research

Study	Label	Conceptualization	Outcome
Reisig et al., 2004	Disrespect	Included verbal indicators of disrespect but excluded all physical acts Operationalization: passive (ignoring officer's commands) or active (name calling, derogatory statements, slurs, and insulting gestures)	When suspects showed disrespect, officers reciprocated with disrespect
Reisig et al., 2004	Disrespect	Included verbal indicators of disrespect but excluded all physical acts Operationalization: passive (ignoring officer's commands) or active (name calling, derogatory statements, slurs, and insulting gestures)	When suspects showed disrespect, officers reciprocated with disrespect
Terrence, 2005	Disrespect	Disrespect was intentionally not conceptualized by researcher	Predicted increase in odds of arrest if juvenile is disrespectful

Table 3. (Continued) Conceptualizations of Disrespect and Outcomes in Recent Research

Study	Label	Conceptualization	Outcome
Novak and Engel, 2005	Disrespectful Demeanor	Conceptualized on two levels: 1. respectful (deferential, civil, or merely passive aggressive) 2. hostility (moderate to high levels of hostility)	Disrespect and hostility increased the likelihood of arrest* * of mentally ill citizens
Terrill and Paoline, 2007	Disrespectful Demeanor	Doing something that showed disrespect to the individual officer or authority of the police officer	Disrespect increased the likelihood of arrest
Dunham and Alpert, 2009	Disrespect	Verbal: swearing or insults Actions: actions including, but not limited to, rolling eyes, disobeying commands, turning away while being spoke to	Officer disrespect toward citizens was more likely when citizen displayed disrespect
Dai et al., 2011	Disrespect	Measured dichotomously with behaviors that were passive aggressive, moderately hostile, and highly hostile	1. Forceful behavior by police reduced likelihood of citizen disrespect. 2. Police disrespect increased likelihood of citizen disrespect

Table 4. Behaviors Forming an Officer-Based Definition of Disrespect

Citizen Behavior	Operational Definition
Impolite or discourteous to officer	Citizen is impolite and it is directed toward/at officer
Verbally antagonistic	Citizen is verbally hostile, belligerent, abusive, or overtly rude
Ignores requests or commands	Citizen is noncompliant, does not follow orders or commands (to move), is completely quiet when asked to respond, or gives no relevant information when asked
Curses/uses profanity	Citizen uses profanity *not* directed toward/at officer
Curses/uses profanity to officer	Citizen uses profanity directed toward/at officer
Makes derogatory statement	Citizen makes derogatory statement directed toward the officer, their family, or in relation to their race
Denies accusations	Citizen denies accusation/wrongdoing for an offense committed in the presence of the officer or for an offense where evidence of guilt is clear to officer
Makes a physical threat to officer	Citizen makes a direct physical threat to officer
Makes an obscene gesture	Citizen makes an obscene gesture toward officer
Takes a defensive/aggressive stance	Citizen takes an aggressive or fighting stance
Spits toward/on officer	Citizen spits on officer or spits in officer's general direction
Attempts escape/flees on foot	Citizen flees from officer on foot prior to or after arrest/detention
Engages in a pursuit	Citizen flees from officer in a vehicle
Physically resists arrest/detention	Citizen physically resists officer's attempt to arrest/detain
Physically assaults officer	Citizen physically assaults officer with hands, feet, or weapon

All but one of the behaviors that officers believed to be disrespectful in Pizio's study have been included in previous conceptualizations but none of these conceptualizations have included all of the behaviors in any single study.[10] In sum, every single causal study has used a different conceptualization of disrespect and even if the individual behaviors examined in these studies are valid indicators, these definitions may not include the full range of behaviors that officers deem to be disrespectful. While Pizio's (2005) results should be taken with caution,[11] the study represented the first research to work toward an officer-based conceptualization of disrespect in the United States.

Definitional issues notwithstanding, the results of the more recent studies have generally confirmed what earlier studies have found. Other than Terrill and Mastrofski (2002) and Terrill (2002), studies have found an increased probability of police sanction when disrespectful behaviors were exhibited (see Engel, 2003; Reisig et al., 2004; Dai et al., 2011). Although not based on actual arrests, Terrence (2005) found that 76% of officers surveyed indicated that they would be more likely to take a juvenile into custody who was disrespectful toward them. Engel and Novak (2005) found that disrespect influenced the probability of arrest of mentally ill citizens while Reisig et al. (2004) found that officers would respond with disrespect when citizens exhibited disrespectful behaviors toward them. It is clear that while exceptions exist, most research continues to find that disrespect does influence the discretionary decisions by officers.

Controlling for Crime in Causal Research

When attempting to understand the influence that extralegal variables have on an officer's decision to arrest, use force, or otherwise sanction a citizen, disrespect and antagonistic demeanor require additional consideration because unlike race or gender for example, the possibility exists that these types of behaviors may also be illegal. Klinger

---

[10] Engaging in a pursuit has not been included in any previous conceptualization.

[11] The study was conducted in only one mid-sized U.S. city with a sample size of 30.

observed that as a construct, 'citizen demeanor' had been defined as: "...legally permissible behavior of citizens during interactions with police officers that indicates the degree of deference or respect they extend to the involved police officers (1994: 477)." He then asserted that previous research was flawed due to the failure to differentiate between criminal and non-criminal behavior in their conceptualizations of demeanor and that criminal behavior was not adequately controlled for in these analyses. In doing so, he raised questions about the validity of findings that citizen demeanor independently influenced police arrest decisions (see also Dunham and Alpert, 2009).

Although it was not his primary goal, Klinger brought attention to the fact that more work in the methodological arena needed to be done. His analysis raised specific concerns which Worden et al. (1996) addressed. Worden et al. reviewed the research and commented on demeanor as a theoretical construct as well as the operationalization of disrespectful demeanor in the research. They stated that Klinger's assertions must not be universally accepted because the research has failed to flush out how officers interpret actions that are both disrespectful and criminal. Worden stated that:

"Actions that are both affronts and crimes can be interpreted in at least two different ways by an officer - as disrespect or as criminal acts - and to stipulate that officers interpret and act on such behavior only in terms of its illegality will obscure rather than illuminate the causal mechanisms we seek to understand; more specifically, we are likely to understate the degree to which officers' decision making is influenced by suspects' demeanor. Thus, the most prudent course for analysis is to distinguish criminal behavior (such as assaults on officers) from legal forms of disrespect and to control for the former in estimating the latter. But... it would be a mistake to categorically exclude illegal acts from a conceptual definition of suspect demeanor" (1996:327).

If examined as a whole, the body of research utilizes valid indicators but the range of behaviors that officers deem to be disrespectful have not been adequately portrayed by any single study. From this it can be concluded that examinations of disrespect must be more than dichotomous variables of civility or hostility and as Klinger asserted, must examine behaviors that could constitute criminal acts. Officers may perceive certain criminal acts such as assault on a police officer or pursuit to be inherently disrespectful and if that is the case, then the suggestion by Worden et al., (1996) to control for the illegal acts while estimating the effects of legal forms of disrespect is both appropriate and warranted. Whether or not officers make decisions based on the criminal offense or the disrespectful behavior is a question for future research but distinguishing exactly what acts officers perceive to be disrespectful and how often they experience them must be understood first.

Limitations of Previous Research

With the bulk of the literature coming from observational studies, two deficiencies are present. First, when researchers themselves formulate and operationalize definitions of disrespect for study, they may not cover the full range of behaviors that officers perceive to be disrespectful. Second, if conceptualizations of disrespect were appropriate, criticism can still be made regarding the reliability of observers in past studies. This is exemplified by Worden and Shepard's (1996) reanalysis of the PSS data where they found that when a citizen's actions were noncompliant or verbally resistant, many observers failed to code these as disrespect.

The question that this brings up is whether or not thirty years of explanatory research in this area has been wrong. It is unlikely. Two possible explanations for these results could be rooted in their definitions of disrespect and force. Unlike previous studies (see for example Engel et al., 2000), Terrill and Mastrofski excluded 'ignoring the officer's commands or requests' (these acts were considered to be passive resistance) and behaviors that were polite (i.e. challenging the officer's authority politely) thus narrowing the range of behaviors that were considered disrespectful (see also Terrill and Paoline, 2007). Secondly, their broad definition of force may have served to mitigate the influence that disrespect had on it (2002).[12]

Regardless of whether the strong criticisms in Klinger's work are correct or misguided, most of the more recent research that has been

---

[12] Their conceptualization of force by officers included acts of physical force, verbal commands, pat-downs, and handcuffing.

published continues to conclude that an independent relationship does exist between suspect disrespect and police decision making, even when taking criminal conduct into account (see for example Mastrofski et al.,1995; Engel et al., 2000; but see Terrill and Mastrofski, 2002). Even so, differing definitions of disrespect utilized in the research continue to be a concern. In the quest for appropriate representations of what officers consider to be disrespectful, researchers have not yet asked officers directly what they deem to be disrespectful, instead focusing on appropriate coding and interpretation via observational research. To make a determination that disrespect does influence police decision-making, we must first have a clear understanding of what the officers themselves perceive as disrespectful. As Worden et al. (1996: 327) noted:

> "Until we learn more about the meaning that police impute to illegal affronts, or unless we are willing to assume that affronts of varying gravity are all equivalent in officers' eyes, we cannot parse out the effect of such affronts to their legal and extralegal dimensions."

Police in the United Kingdom

Introduction

The police in the U.K. are not so different than police in the U.S. Their crime control goals and functions are similar as is their method of policing (see Bayley, 1985; Waddington, 1999a). They have parallel powers of arrest and detention (see Dammer and Fairchild, 2006) and they both have seen public support rise and fall with occurrences of alleged police misconduct such as the Abner Louima or Amadou Diallo incidents in New York City and the Stephen Lawrence murder investigation and the Holloway Road incident in London.[13] In sum,

---

[13] In 1997, Louima was arrested by officers at a bar fight. He was then brought to the police station, was beaten and was sodomized by officers. Amadou Diallo was shot by four police officers in 1999. Although cleared of misconduct, the incident sparked outrage against the NYPD. In 1993, Stephen Lawrence was murdered and the resulting investigation was alleged to be rife with institutional racism and incompetence (see Shiner 2010). The Holloway Road incident refers to an encounter in 1983 where a special unit

officers and police encounters in both of these developed countries are similar and any differences that do exist between the two countries may have more to do with the culture and the citizens of each country than the role of the police. As they are in the U.S., most police encounters in the U.K. are cordial and are completed without any unfavorable behaviors from either party (Waddington, 1999a). Even in law enforcement and arrest situations where the officer's authoritative role is clearly identifiable, there is little evidence to suggest that antagonism or disrespect is a normal occurrence. There is some evidence that citizens display disrespectful behaviors at times and that officers may respond negatively, however that is based more on anecdotal evidence than empirical research (see Weinberger, 1995). The research that does exist in this area focuses more on citizen dissatisfaction with police and how citizens are more likely to formally complain than informally express dissatisfaction during the encounter itself.

This section will focus on the interactions between citizens and the police in the U.K. The nature of police-citizen encounters will be examined first followed by a review of the research into extra-legal factors that influence police decision-making. Finally, the limitations of the extant research will be addressed.

The Nature of Police-Citizen Encounters

In both the U.S. and the U.K., the majority of police officers are on regular patrol (Bayley, 1994). They walk or drive around, engage in pro-active crime control, and respond to service and law enforcement related calls. While a small percentage of their time is actually engaged in crime fighting activity, patrol officers are still out on the streets communicating with the public every day (Bayley, 1985; Fields and Moore, 1996; Newburn, 2008).

It is logical to presume that officers in the U.K. engage in a higher percentage of voluntary encounters with citizens due to the fact that foot patrol is much more prominent in the U.K. In London, it is much more common to see foot patrol constables/officers and police

---

of the London Metropolitan Police beat a group of youths who had exhibited disrespect toward the officers.

community support officers than it is in metropolitan areas in the U.S.[14] Moreover, the system of policing in the U.K. has embraced neighborhood policing which is more citizen focused and emphasizes more approachable and accessible police forces and officers. This is not to say that officers in vehicles or on foot patrol assignments will shy away from law enforcement related encounters. Given the increase in violent crime and "hooliganism,"[15] police management in the U.K. recognizes the need to retain their law enforcement role. Instead, it must be understood that police in the U.K. and especially London place a strong organizational priority on community policing along with their crime control function (see Scott, 1998; Yates et al., 2001; Neyroud 2009; London Metropolitan Police, 2011).

Partly in response to decreasing public confidence in police, the National Policing Improvement Agency (NPIA) was formed in 2007 (NPIA, 2010). This new agency's over-riding goal is to increase police efficiency by seeking to link the day-to-day realities and activities of police to evidence. Within this larger goal, the NPIA is tasked to examine the restructuring of the police to improve performance and allow for a stronger focus on neighborhood policing (see Neyroud, 2009). By assessing the levels of anti-social behavior and disorder in neighborhoods (see Moore 2011), the agency hopes to identify emerging and effective practices to enhance order and public confidence through their Safer Neighbourhoods initiative (NPIA, 2010).

---

[14] Police community support officers are non-sworn civilians who are only on foot patrol. They are in uniform and are assigned to a specific area or neighborhood along with a sworn officer but have no powers of arrest or detention. Their primary purpose is to assist in bridging the gap between the community and the police by assisting citizens and being a visible non-enforcement arm of the London Metropolitan Police.

[15] "Hooliganism" refers to the violence at soccer matches involving hundreds/thousands of fans. These situations have become more violent and more prevalent and the police have been consistently criticized for their handling of these incidents, especially in those where deaths have occurred (see Fields and Moore, 1996).

This organizational priority and formation of the NPIA are also supported by a small body of research that has examined the public's view of police. Drawing from the 2003/2004 British Crime Survey and the 2006/2007 London Metropolitan Police Safer Neighbourhoods Survey, Jackson and Bradford (2009) found that citizens see police as supporters and facilitators of social cohesion and moral consensus rather than having the more narrow law enforcement viewpoint. Jackson and Sunshine (2007) concurred, finding that the public saw the police role as enforcers of social order and cohesion, rather than crime. Bradford (2011:15) went further and suggested that people in the U.K. "value how they are treated as individuals, albeit as individuals who sit within the broader structures the police may still represent." Given these results, it is understandable why police in the U.K. have moved toward a more community oriented policing model which places a strong emphasis on the quality of life of its citizens.

     Not all agree that quality of life should be such an important part of policing and more generally, public policy. Crawford (2009) argues that criminal justice and regulation are "awkward bedfellows" and that regulation is being used to "circumvent and undermine" criminal justice principles (2009: 810-811). He goes on to state that this focus may formalize previously informal governmental outcomes and give police the right to intervene based on behavior that is merely anti-social rather than criminal.

     Crawford's criticisms notwithstanding, the organizational emphasis on community policing and quality of life does not diminish the control and authority that officers must initially put forth and maintain in citizen encounters. Like police officers in the U.S., officers in the U.K. enter into encounters believing that they are in the dominant and authoritative position. They exercise their power to stop and search (see Waddington et al., 2004) and within those interactions, they structure conversations around their concerns, are expected to display certainty, and demand deference (Waddington, 1999a).

     This is not unreasonable given their position as police officers but even so, their demand for deference is muted by the norms of their civil and non-confrontational culture (see Fox, 2005). The relative homogeneity of the U.K. (compared to the U.S.) allows participants to have a better understanding of what behavior is expected of them in encounters (see Charon, 2001). While it is unacceptable for officers in both countries to abuse their authority, British officers are also not allowed to 'act with incivility' when in encounters with citizens (Waddington, 1999a) and unlike officers in the U.S., U.K. police officers may be seen as the defenders of public values and behavioral norms (Jackson and Bradford, 2009). Bradford (2011) agreed and stated that support for the police may be relate more to social cohesion and the reduction of disorder than crime.

This social cohesion aspect is implied by Waddington (2008: 469), who further stated that the public has found uses of physical force to become increasingly unacceptable and that they have concerns about officers' "extracting a measure of summary justice..." when they see officers using force. This is partially due to the rare nature of uses of force in the U.K. as well as the non-confrontational aspect of cultural norms in the U.K. So even though the legitimate capacity to use force is a defining characteristic of police in the U.K. (and U.S.), it is still viewed as problematic in the U.K. (Waddington, 2008).

The cultural norms coupled with the organizational mandate results in police-citizen encounters that are more civil and less aggressive from both parties but as Waddington (1999a) stated, the cordial behavior from police officers relies on the members of the public and more importantly, their deference. If they refuse to obey the officer or challenge the officer's authority, a coercive and authoritative response from the officer will follow (1999a). That being said, just how the officer would react to disrespect or the lack of deference is unknown. While the probability of arrest increases as offense seriousness increases (Scott, 1998), there is still a possibility that extra-legal factors such as disrespect influence arrest decisions. However, to date, no study of policing in the U.K. has addressed this.

The Influence of Disrespect on Police Decision Making: The Lack of Empirical Research

Given the similarities related to both role and function of police in these two countries, it is interesting that there is no research that has examined the impact of citizen behavior on decisions to arrest or use physical force. There is a body of research that examines police-citizen encounters, confidence in the police, and police decision making in the U.K but much of that research assesses police stop and search practices in relation to suspect race (see for example Waddington et al., 2004; Delsol and Shiner, 2006; Jackson et al., 2009; Shiner, 2010). A smaller body of research does address public confidence and citizen dissatisfaction with the way police act in encounters but that research does not address the behavior of citizens, disrespectful or not. It would be unreasonable to assume that all police-citizen encounters in the U.K. are completed without some dissatisfaction on the part of either participant and so it is surprising that researchers have not fully ventured into this arena. While little empirical research exists, it is known that police in the U.K. experience similar criticisms as their U.S. counterparts, especially in relation to stop and search (Delsol and Shiner, 2006; Shiner, 2011). It is also known that these encounters are a significant source of dissatisfaction, especially among minorities (Delsol and Shiner, 2006).

In 1999, the MacPherson Report revealed a trend of institutional racism and racial profiling by the London Metropolitan Police. While only a small portion of the report was relegated to police stop and search, its findings intensified and reinforced negative views from minorities (Waddington et al., 2004; see also Shiner, 2011). In fact, Miller (2010) found that the reform efforts of the MacPherson Report have had little effect on the disproportionate searches of minorities in London.[16] This may help explain why minorities have held consistently less favorable views of officers and are less satisfied with police service, especially when they contact the police with a crime problem (Dammer and Fairchild, 2006; Miller, 2010). While this problem parallels what is occurring in the U.S., citizens in the U.K., including minority citizens, are less likely to confront officers directly.

Instead, the research suggests that citizens are more likely to express their dissatisfaction by making formal complaints to the respective police department (Walters and Brown, 2000). In their survey research, Walters and Brown (2000) found that although some respondents perceived a lack of respect from officers, most indicated that dissatisfaction with officers' behaviors was primarily due to officers' lacking empathy or questioning the legitimacy of their story. Moreover, many citizens felt dissatisfied with the process rather than the individual officer (see also Maguire and Corbett, 1991; Jackson et

---

[16] Although Miller did examine data from 38 English police forces and found that the disproportionate searches in London weighed heavily on his findings.

al., 2010). This suggests that even if citizens in the U.K. feel dissatisfied with police service or perceive that an officer has not treated them with respect, it may not necessarily lead to a disrespectful reaction from them. In short, the civil nature of interpersonal relations in the U.K. in general may lead citizens to formally complain later rather than react to the police behavior during the encounter (see Maguire and Corbett,1991; Walters and Brown, 2000; Fox, 2005).[17]

It is inevitable that police in the U.K. will encounter disrespectful citizens as a function of the job itself yet little is known in relation to how they perceive or define disrespect, and if their experiences are different than officers in the U.S. Weinberger (1995) and Brogden (1991) asserted that officers did respond with force when faced with disrespectful citizens but those assertions were based solely on oral histories. A study of the police complaints system (prior to the 2002 legislation) found that citizens resist officers by failing to defer to the officer's authority and that these citizens behaviorally expressed a lack of deference by being impolite or verbally antagonistic (Maguire and Corbett, 1991). These few studies indicate some similarity with U.S. research but without more empirical evidence, it is unknown how British police officers define citizen disrespect, how often it occurs, and how they respond to it when it does (see Newburn, 2008).

Limitations of Prior Research

Based on an examination of the current body of evidence, it is clear that a major gap in the literature exists. While it is generally agreed upon that police decisions in both countries are based more on contextual factors (see Worden, 1998; Waddington, 1999b), this assertion in the U.K. has not been supported by the empirical evidence. The lack of support however, is based solely on the lack of relevant research rather than the presence of research with contrary findings. Furthermore, the lack of research is surprising given the role and function of police in the

---

[17] Given the overhaul of the police complaints system resulting in 2002 legislation improving the way police handle citizen complaints, one would expect a body of research focusing on the complaint system itself. Unfortunately, there have been surprisingly few studies (see McLaughlin and Johansen, 2006).

U.K and the findings that suggest that some citizens are dissatisfied with the way police behave during encounters.

In a developed country where public support and confidence for police has declined during the past decade (see Bowling et al., 2008; Reiner, 2008; Jackson and Bradford, 2009; Bradford 2011), it is important to understand what factors influence encounters as they progress. It is crucial that future policing research in the U.K. address the extra-legal factors that may influence police decision-making. With disrespect being one of those extra-legal factors, it is also important to understand how officers see certain behaviors and how they determine what behaviors are affronts to themselves personally or their occupation as a police officer. The lack of research examining this aspect of policing leaves a clear gap in the literature that this research can begin to fill.

Organizational Differences

Certainly, the situational predictors of police behavior as well as the structure and function of departments are important to examine. That being said, one must also address any organizational differences that may exist when comparing police departments. Since individual police organizations may vary on numerous levels (see Maguire and Uchida, 2000), any differences that are found could be due to formal or informal characteristics of the organization rather than historical, structural, or functional differences that may exist. Moreover, while police are somewhat isolated from the public and political culture, it is clear that these external forces also influence organizations. So when comparing two distinct police organizations, it is important to take into account how organizational characteristics influence what police organizations do and what they are.

A growing body of empirical work has focused on what police organizations are as well as how to compare them for study. Starting with Wilson (1968), a strong body of research began to focus on organizational differences related to the structures of different police departments. Wilson examined organizational structures and political environments and how they related to patterns of police behavior (1968). Using Wilson's work as their foundation, later studies examined organizational differences in police agencies and found that both internal and external forces influence police organizations (see for example Manning, 1977; Langworthy, 1985; see also Maguire, 2003 for a review).

The more recent trend in organizational research in policing follows from this tradition by moving away from studies that focus on organizational structure and more towards research that focuses on the environment(s) that police organizations operate in. Whether it be the resources available to police organizations, outside pressure to engage in crime fighting or community policing, or the focus on the external environment that police work in, each organization may be influenced and may respond in different fashions. For example, a department's philosophy on community policing and operational strategies to achieve a level of community policing could influence deployment and officer behavior (see Cordner, 2005). Additionally, the jurisdictions or neighborhoods in which officers work influence how they behave (see Terrill and Reisig, 2003).[18]

Most policing research focuses primarily on the situations police work in and how situational factors influence the behaviors of individual officers (see for example Worden, 1995). Given this, the body of literature examining how police organizations influence decision making at the officer level is lacking and as a result, little is known about what formal and informal organizational characteristics influence officers' decisions (See Sherman, 1980; Riksheim and Chermak, 1993; Maguire, 2003). It is both time consuming and methodologically difficult to study organizations and the inability of organizational theory to adequately and consistently explain police decisions may be more due to methodological difficulties than the predictors themselves. Maguire (2003:46) summed the state of research by stating:

"The concept of organizational environment is the great snafu of organization science. The discovery of its importance was one of the greatest achievements in the study of organizations, but conquering its overall complexity remains one of the greatest challenges."

---

[18] While some research has been conducted focusing on police organizations and the environment they work in, organizational research still falls short in the effort to explain police decisions (see Worden, 1995).

Of particular importance to this study is the relationship of departmental size as an organizational characteristic and how that may influence officers' perceptions and interpretations of specific (disrespectful) citizen behaviors. In the U.S., McDevitt and Baum (1996) surveyed police chiefs from various size departments and found striking similarity with strategies to fight and reduce crime by focusing on juveniles. Apart from McDevitt and Baum's work, Maguire and Uchida's (2000) review of past studies found that the influence of organizational size was a consistent predictor in that it influenced the style, structure, and processes of specific departments. In the present study, if the difference in departmental size influences the style of policing and/or the structures of the departments, it could also influence how officers are trained and socialized in relation to dealing with citizens.

Wilson's assertions about political context must also be revisited as they relate to this research. Wilson (1968) asserted that the political environment influences police organizations and behavior. It must be recognized that the political environment in the U.S. is significantly different than in the U.K., and London in specific. Moreover, cultural differences themselves may influence how a police department operates. Unfortunately, the research in the U.K. in this area is even more limited than in the U.S. Other than a handful of studies that have examined institutional racism in the MET after the MacPherson Report[19] (see also Waddington et al., 2004; Delsol and Shiner, 2006; Miller, 2010), little is known about how organizational characteristics of the MET influence police decision-making.

Based on the above, it is clear that there is a lack of available literature in both countries in relation to organizational characteristics and how they influence police behavior. What research is present in the U.S. points to how departmental size and structure may influence police behavior. Keeping this in mind, it must be stated that international comparisons of police organizations show similarities in relation to organizational structure and levels of decentralization (Mawby and Wright, 2008). Even with this, it must be recognized that

---

[19] The MacPherson Report examined trends of institutional racism and racial profiling within the MET after the unsolved murder of Stephen Lawrence, a young black male.

the size of each organization and the external factors that impact each organization could influence officers' perceptions of disrespect. Since the present research cannot control for these factors, the comparative results must be viewed with caution. Organizational difference notwithstanding, there is a clear gap in the literature that this research seeks to fill. In the U.S., the research reveals a consistent direct relationship between disrespect and police sanctioning. In the U.K., the research shows that citizens experience dissatisfaction with officers but they are less likely to act disrespectfully in the officer's presence, even if that officer has acted disrespectfully toward them. In both countries, officers see themselves as authoritative figures during all interactions with citizens and as such, they warrant respect and deference from those citizens. When a citizen fails to show deference and acts disrespectfully, the possibility exists that officers will sanction that citizen but prior any causal analyses or any cross-national comparison, it is crucial to understand how officers themselves define disrespect in each country.

Chapter 3

Statement of and Rationale for the Hypotheses

Introduction

Like all interactions between people, police encounters with citizens include elements or factors which bring unpredictability and uncertainty into those encounters.

To put it differently, how officers act and react in encounters with citizens will be influenced by the values, customs, and practices of the organization that the participants are a part of as well as the characteristics of a given encounter with a citizen.

Given this, it cannot be assumed that police interactions among and between officers in each country will proceed in an identical fashion. Hence, it is necessary to understand those values, customs, and practices when studying interactions in two distinct cultures when attempting to discern how police interpret citizen behaviors and how they respond to them. In this chapter, historical, occupational (function/role), officer, and country differences will be addressed to help justify the specific hypotheses.

This chapter is organized in the following way. The hypotheses for model testing related to the anticipation and perception of armed officers in the U.K. (compared only to unarmed U.K. officers) will be assessed in relation to the historical differences between the police in the two countries. Looking next to the differences in the police role and function in the two countries, rationales for the hypotheses related to productivity and cynicism will be addressed. The hypotheses focusing officer's differences will then be discussed and justified. The last section presents a discussion of the differences of norms and customs between the two countries with the objective of justifying the hypotheses related to anticipation and definitional inclusivity. A summary of the formal hypotheses for the research will appear at the end of this chapter.

Historical Differences

Armed Officers

From the birth of formal police to modern day policing in both countries, the presence or absence of guns in these countries is one of the primary characteristics that set them apart. The U.K. is a predominately weaponless society and their homicide rate reflects this. In 2006, gun-related homicides accounted for only 6.6% of the 755 homicides (Home Office, 2007). This is in sharp contrast to the 76% of homicides in the U.S. that were committed with firearms in 2006 (FBI, 2007). Given the history of an unarmed police force and the low rate of gun crime, many officers in the U.K. have no interest in becoming a firearms officer and even have difficulty imagining what it is like to carry a weapon on duty.

When thinking back to the formation of the police in the U.K., having an unarmed police force was crucial in Sir Robert Peel's effort to moderate the power imbalance between police and citizens and to avoid the formidable appearance that a firearm would symbolize (Waddington and Wright, 2008). Peel made a conscious political decision to distance the police from the military and not arming the police was the most visible expression of this decision (2008; Emsley, 2008; see also Waddington and Wright 2010). Today, the MET does employ a small percentage of officers who carry firearms but the MET still remains a primarily unarmed police force.

As of June 30, 2007, the MET employed 30,996 police officers with only 2581 (8.3%) listed as authorized firearms officers (Lister, 2007). The function of the Specialist Firearms Command of the MET is to respond to serious encounters where a weapon might be present. Even if a patrol vehicle with unarmed officers is one block away when a call of this nature goes out, regulations force those officers to divert without hesitation, even if an armed response vehicle (ARV) is further away. In London, armed officers are not assigned to foot patrol Given the low percentage of armed officers and the low incidence of violent crime where the suspect is believed to have a weapon, it is unusual for a citizen to encounter an armed officer and for an officer to encounter an armed citizen.

When an armed British police officer does arrive at an encounter, their firearm signifies that 'formidable appearance' that Peel was working to avoid when the MET was initially formed. These armed officers present a significant departure from the majority of officers with whom citizens engage in encounters. Arming a small percentage of officers in an unarmed police force is a significant "...assertion of the seriousness with which such decisions are taken" (Waddington, 1993: 238) and thus a recognition that the presence of a firearm could likely influence how a citizen will react to the armed officer. Even though armed U.K. officers are the only officers called to serious encounters where weapons might be present, it is reasonable to assert that those police officers who enter into these encounters would identify these situations as more dire or serious and would be more conscious of behaviors that are outside the bounds of acceptability.

While these officers would be more conscious of possible disrespectful behaviors, it can still be hypothesized that they will experience disrespect less often than their unarmed counterparts. Citizens in the U.K. are unaccustomed to having a firearm in their presence, even when that firearm is worn by a police officer. While armed U.K. officers can be called to non-serious offenses/calls, citizens are more likely to encounter unarmed officers given that less than 10% of the MET's officers carry a firearm. In situations where an armed officer is called to, the suspect's attention becomes drawn to the weapon and this attention may lead the suspect to appreciate the seriousness of the encounter which in turn would reduce the probability that they may act disrespectfully. In short, the firearm becomes a factor that could influence a citizen's behavior. Accordingly, suspects become more aware of their own conduct and should curtail their behavior to comport with the officer's commands. Furthermore, it can be expected that armed officers would enter into potentially violent and non-violent encounters with a more cautious and authoritative approach. When entering into encounters with an authoritative demeanor and a weapon that represents an added observable demonstration of authority, the citizens these officers encounter may see the weapon as a significant element of that encounter. As such, the presence of a firearm may lead citizens to have a more pronounced perception their subservient role, thus promoting compliance.

In this instance, one cannot ignore the fact that armed officers in the U.K. are those who deal with violent and possibly armed criminals. While this possibility exists, serious encounters where weapons might be present still have a low probability that the weapon in question will be a firearm. Moreover, it is reasonable to expect that encounters such as these in the U.K. still have the cultural dimension of civility to them, a dimension that might not be as prevalent in the U.S.

Conversely, all police officers are armed in the U.S. and it is estimated that 57 million U.S. residents own guns (Hepburn et al., 2007). So while an officer's gun symbolizes authority in the U.S., it is much more commonplace and may become just another symbol akin to a patrol car, badge, and uniform. As such, a suspect in the U.S. may not pay special attention to the officer's weapon given that every police officer they have seen has carried a gun.

Being able to compare the effect of weapons on the perception or anticipation of disrespect between officers in these two countries could yield interesting results. Unfortunately, the current sample does not allow for analysis due to the fact that all U.S. police officers in this sample carry a sidearm. Accordingly, the analysis will be restricted to comparing armed and unarmed officers in the U.K.

Based on the above discussion, two hypotheses are generated:

H$_1$: Armed police officers in the U.K. will be less likely to experience disrespect than unarmed police officers in the U.K.

H$_2$: Armed police officers in the U.K will be less likely to anticipate disrespect than unarmed police officers in the U.K.

Differences in the Police Role and Function

The literature supports the notion that police in different countries function similarly. In the U.S. and U.K., the stated police function revolves around law enforcement and officers have a great deal of power, wide discretion, and relative autonomy from their organization (see Waddington, 1993; Bayley, 1994; Newburn, 2008). Informally, public opinion rises and falls with occurrences of police bravery and misconduct (Miller and Davis, 2008; Newburn, 2008). Moreover, police solidarity remains an ever-present facet of the police occupation (in the U.K., see Reiner, 1992; Westmarland, 2008. In the U.S., see

Skolnick and Fyfe, 1993). In short, men and women who become police officers are socialized into the group or family of police officers and this group becomes the primary source for their viewpoint. While the characteristics of police subculture may vary from department to department, Skolnick (2008) asserted that certain features are universal, stable, and lasting. These universal characteristics of police subculture focus on the development of a strong bond with other officers and an identity based on police function, solidarity, and authority. The identity that is created stems from the formation of two distinct relationships. The first is the relationship formed among officers. Through the law enforcement-based police function and relative isolation from the citizenry they serve, officers become a cohesive group with an identity that is lodged in the institutional setting. How officers see themselves is channeled by the organizations in which they're embedded and their actions reflect that group identity. Simply put, the police occupation is one of the only ones where the institutional identity revolves around danger and authority (see Skolnick, 1966) and this subculture helps characterize the outlook and viewpoint in which officers perceive encounters with citizens and suspects.

Until more recently, Westmarland (2008: 253) suggested that police culture has been described as a singular 'one size fits all.' However, there is a growing realization that the influence of officer characteristics does influence police cultures and that this may vary from culture to culture as well (2008). It would be a mistake to think that individuals have only one viewpoint or outlook, and as such, that must be tempered with the understanding that the uniqueness of the police role leads officers to feel as if their identity is based primarily within the authoritative role of their occupation.

This identity also guides the second distinct relationship, the one between officers and citizens. This 'us versus them' relationship is characterized by distrust, cynicism, separation, and expected subservience from citizens (see for example Skolnick, 1966; Skolnick and Fyfe, 1993; Westmarland, 2008). In much the same way, the bonding of police officers and creation of a police subculture also leads to a clear and marked separation from citizens. Most encounters with police officers are involuntary in nature and by means of their appearance and commands, officers inform citizens of the subservience they are expected to display. All officers in the U.S. and some in the

U.K. have patrol vehicles and weapons as additional symbols. Coupled with an officer's commands, it is clear to citizens that officers will be the authoritative figure in encounters and that citizens should exercise deference and compliance. When citizens do not yield to that authority and act disrespectfully, they move outside the bounds of acceptable behavior.

In addition, officers may see encounters with criminal suspects or arrestees differently than non-law enforcement related encounters. They may see suspects as 'symbolic assailants' (Skolnick, 1966) and that perception may shift their behavior to become more authoritative, causing them to anticipate disrespect or to be more conscious of potentially disrespectful behaviors. In short, the police role and the separation from citizens guides interactions and announces officers to citizens in a way that informs them how the officers will act and how citizens should act in return.

When thinking about the role of police and the thin blue line that separates police from citizens, these relationships are important to understand. While the hypotheses outlined below predict that differences exist, they do so within the context of an officer's identity that is lodged in an institutional setting, that of being a police officer. So the differences that are hypothesized are not due to varying degrees of solidarity in the two countries but due to the differences in police function and the citizens they police.

Productivity

As noted above, the police identity is based within an officer's perspective but it does not imply that all officers will see and interpret all situations and citizen/suspect behaviors in the same manner. To an extent, productivity is an element of acceptance by one's police peers. Aggressive, highly productive officers differentiate themselves from low-productivity officers and are universally admired and heavily rewarded (Toch, 1995). While other factors do exist (i.e. the willingness to use force when called upon to do so), social acceptance into the group can be a product of how pro-active the officer is or how much law enforcement-related work the officer is willing to get involved with.

In a sense, variation will exist partly due to factors associated with the police function. For example, it can be hypothesized that productive officers in both countries will have a higher probability of encountering disrespectful citizens than officers who are less productive. While it's logical to suppose that productive officers[20] will experience more disrespect simply because they are involved with more involuntary encounters, it is more complicated than that.

There is a logical connection then between an officer's level of productivity, how those officers perceive their role, and how they characterize situations that they enter into. If officers perceive their role as primarily law enforcers, it is logical to assert that they would be pro-active and would spend more time engaged in crime fighting activities. This focus on crime fighting activity can also lead to higher levels of cynicism and even use of force. For example, Worden (1995) found some support for the assertion that officers who conceive their role in narrow crime fighting terms (excluding public nuisances and personal problems) are more likely to use force.

From this, it is logical to assume that given similar situations and types of encounters, these productive officers would be more likely to experience disrespect from citizens. If they have perceived disrespect in similar types of encounters, it is reasonable to assume that those experiences would hold over and influence present situations. So if an officer has been involved in more law enforcement-based encounters where they have experienced disrespectful citizen behavior, they will remember those past experiences and this may lead them to go into those types of encounters expecting disrespectful behavior. An officer's prior experiences may also lead them to form conclusions that citizens are acting disrespectfully, even if it was the officer's aggression that prompted the disrespect in the first place.

From the above discussion, it can be hypothesized that a positive relationship exists between the level of productivity of U.S. and U.K. officers and the probability that officers will experience disrespect from citizens. That being said, it can also be hypothesized that productive officers in the U.S. will have a higher probability of experiencing disrespect than productive officers in the U.K. In the U.K., there has been a strong focus on public order policing and while that focus is balanced with law enforcement based priorities (see Willis, 2005),

---

[20] Productivity is defined as officers who have a self-reported higher number of arrests compared to their peers.

officers in the U.K. still seek to maintain civility and appropriate behavior during interactions. While maintaining civility in encounters with criminal suspects is not unheard of in either country, it is asserted here that the politeness and civility of productive officers in the U.K. will likely result in similar behaviors and reactions from criminal suspects. Simply put, the conduct of both participants in police-suspect encounters in the U.K. will reflect this aspect of English culture, compared to police-suspect encounters in the U.S. As such, U.K. officers who are more productive (via the amount of arrests they make) are less likely to perceive disrespect from citizens and suspects than productive U.S. officers.

Based on the above discussion, two hypotheses are generated:

H₃: In both countries, productive police officers will have a higher probability of experiencing disrespect than police officers who are less productive.

H₄: Productive police officers in the U.S. will have a higher probability of experiencing disrespect than productive police officers in the U.K.

Cynicism

The above hypotheses that assert differences between officers in these two countries are based primarily on cultural norms and historical differences between police in the two countries rather than differences in the perspectives of the officers themselves. Certainly there are few who would argue against the presence of a police subculture and the literature supports this notion, as noted above. The implication brings one back to the distinct relationship shared by officers and how that relationship influences situations that officers and citizens are in.

The police subculture is characterized by a strong bond between officers and a cynical, distrusting view of citizens and suspects (see Skolnick, 1966; Skolnick and Fyfe, 1993; Waddington, 1993). These elements lead to social isolation (from both citizens and police administrators), police solidarity, and what Skolnick and Fyfe (1993) called an 'us versus them' state of mind. Waddington (1993) further asserted that cynicism is a good defense strategy for officers in the U.K., implying that they will rarely be disappointed when they go into encounters expecting the worst from citizens, especially in the face of decreasing public confidence (also see Shiner, 2010). Worden (1995) asserted that cynical American officers are those who view citizens negatively and believe that citizens do not respect the police. His research even found modest support for the contention that cynical officers are more likely to use force (1995). Like varying levels of productivity however, it cannot be assumed that all officers maintain the same level of cynicism. Given differences related to officers, departments, and cultures, it is reasonable to assert that all officers will not move through the exact same interpretive process. While the subculture they are a part of may shape their outlook, there are other factors that will as well, as noted above. In the simplest of terms, different officers have different experiences (in life and on the job) and some may be more cynical towards citizens than others.

Cynical officers are likely to enter into situations having already assumed that the citizen or suspect will lie or attempt to deceive them. They will seek subservience but will not expect that they'll receive it. This will shape how they interact with citizens and even if they are the ones who become aggressive at the outset, a comparable reaction from a citizen will further support the officer's contention that the citizen is being disrespectful. Accordingly, it can be argued that cynical officers in both countries would experience more disrespect from citizens than those who are less cynical.

Based on the above discussion, one hypothesis is generated:

H5: In both countries, cynical police officers will experience more disrespect from citizens than police officers who less cynical.

Officer Differences

Are cops the same the world over or will they differ in how they see and interpret citizen behavior in police-citizen encounters? To support the (general) assertion that police are the same the world over, one could focus on how strong the police subculture is and how the reference group for officers is other officers, not the citizens they're serving. If the actions of an officer speak for the police in general rather than the individual, one could expect that discretionary decision-making by police would be consistent among different officers. The literature makes clear that this is not the case and that variation does exist in officer decision-making (see Worden, 1995). Even though an officer's occupational perspective can be firmly embedded in the police subculture, it cannot be the only perspective that the officer will draw from. In short, due to its unique nature, the individuality of humans cannot be ignored. This assertion is supported by Westmarland (2008) who stated that the police subculture in different organizations varies and some of that variation stems from officer differences. Moreover, when assessing officers' perceptions of disrespect and its influence in police-citizen encounters, it is important to be aware of the demographic characteristics of police officers and how they might influence such encounters. For example, age, experience, level of education, gender, and race are all characteristics that could influence how officers perceive disrespectful behaviors from citizens.

Age and Experience

Older, more experienced officers have, by definition, experienced more. They become comfortable with the job and it is logical to speculate that they have a better understanding of the citizens that they deal with. While it could be argued that with more time comes a diminished ability to see the citizen's viewpoint, it can be asserted that these officers may experience fewer disrespectful citizens or encounters since they have a better understanding of how to deal with certain situations through years of experience. For example, older, more experienced officers may be more adept at and willing to utilize de-escalation techniques when confronted by a disrespectful citizen. Conversely, younger, less experienced officers may respond aggressively which may serve to intensify encounters thereby increasing the probability that citizens will begin or continue to be disrespectful. Having time on the job makes it easier for experienced officers to work in a cooperative effort with citizens.

When seeking to process and end interactions in a safe manner, that cooperative effort is crucial, even if arrest is the intended outcome. In arrest situations, the tenets of officer safety specify that they should have full control of the suspect, regardless of whether that control is physical or psychological. So if the outcome is not what the citizen would choose (i.e. arrest, ticket) and this is verbally expressed to the officer, that officer will make clear that the outcome could be even less desirable if the citizen continues in the direction they are going (see van Maanen, 1974). This could be in the form of a calm command, stern warning, or threat of physical force. Older, more experienced officers are better equipped to react toward citizens in a more civil manner. This is because they take their past experiences into account and become more deliberate when working toward their goal. As a result, they work to reach their goal in a more inquisitorial rather than adversarial fashion and understand that arresting or using physical force based on behavior committed during the interaction may be a more difficult or problematic route to take. For example, it would be logical to assume a forty or fifty-year-old officer would want to communicate with rather than fight or run after a twenty-year-old suspect. It is clear that one can convey authority without being aggressive and that the language used during interactions can shape the process and methods used by officers in those interactions.

This form of interaction also allows the citizen to understand and possibly respect the older and more experienced officer compared to the younger, less experienced officer who may be focused on performance and productivity. As a result, a citizen's behavior would be more likely to conform to the officer's expectations of subservience. Although younger, less experienced officers make more arrests and are involved in more use of force situations (see Terrill, 2001; Williams and Hester, 2001; but also see Worden, 1995), it does not necessarily suggest that older, more experienced officers shy away from work and arrests. Instead, they have a better understanding of how to communicate in an effective way so that they may reach their goals without force or aggression. Given this, citizens will exhibit less disrespectful behavior during these interactions and when officers do perceive disrespect, they have the ability to reach their outcome goal without being influenced by disrespectful behaviors that may occur during the interaction itself.

Based on the above discussion, two hypotheses are generated:

H$_6$: In both countries, police officers who are older will experience disrespect less often than younger police officers.

H_7: In both countries, police officers who are more experienced will experience disrespect less often than less experienced police officers.

Level of Education

This assertion may apply to educated officers as well. Educated officers may come onto the job with stronger communication skills and a better appreciation for conflict resolution based on their academic and social experiences. Even though an officer's level of education is not known by the citizen, the officers will use those social and educational experiences to keep situations calm and to de-escalate situations when they move towards volatility. Educated officers may be more deliberative when solving problems and working toward goals, and may be more attuned to the different social and cultural backgrounds of citizens. This is especially true in London and larger U.S. cities where populations are more diverse. During these encounters, educated officers may intentionally use language and communication skills to demonstrate empathy or understanding in an effort to calm citizens. Like officers who are older or more experienced, educated officers may be better equipped to communicate based on their past experiences, even if those experiences occurred in the classroom instead of on the job.

In turn, the citizens they encounter may see these interactions as ones where they do not perceive a need to be disrespectful and even when they do, an officer's conflict resolution skills could be beneficial in diffusing those situations. As a result, educated officers have been found to receive fewer citizen complaints (Cohen and Chaiken, 1972) and are more likely to use reasonable force (rather than excessive force) when the need for it arises (Worden, 1995). Based on this, it is reasonable to assert that officers from both countries who have a higher level of education will perceive disrespect less often in police-citizen encounters.

Based on the above discussion, one hypothesis is generated:

H_8: In both countries, more educated police officers will experience disrespect less often than less educated police officers.

Race and Gender

If a citizen was asked to describe the demographics of a typical police officer, they would probably describe the officer as being a white male. This is not unreasonable given that most officers fit that description. In 2003, females accounted for 11.3% of officers in the U.S. nationwide and 14.6% of police officers in police departments serving populations between 250,000 and 499,999 (Pastore and Maguire, 2006). In London, females accounted for 20.6% of all officers in the MET (Clegg and Kirwan, 2006) and in the entire U.K., women represent 22% of all police officers (Office of National Statistics, 2007). While the proportion of female officers in both countries continues to rise, citizens are still more likely to encounter a male officer.

In regards to race, white police officers accounted for 76.4% of officers in the U.S. as a whole and 66.6% of officers in departments serving populations between 250,000 and 499,999 (Pastore and Maguire, 2006). In London, white officers accounted for 94.4% of all officers in the MET (Clegg and Kirwan, 2006) and 96.3% of all officers in the U.K. (Office of National Statistics, 2007). Based on the statistics offered above, it is clear that citizens in both countries are more likely to encounter a white male officer.

Race relations in U.S. have been problematic throughout history and the relationship between the police and minorities has been at the forefront. In regards to the influence of race on police decision-making, most of the existing literature has focused on the race of citizens and suspects, and how their race influences officers' discretionary decisions. Although public opinion polls in the U.S. regularly indicate that blacks have lower levels of favorability and believe that police use more force against blacks (Pastore and Maguire, 2006), empirical research regarding the influence of citizen race on officer decision making has been inconsistent at best.[21]

In the U.K., the police are also criticized for their treatment of minority citizens. Minorities hold negative views and are generally less

---

[21] For more information on this topic, please see the following studies: Studies that have found that race does influence the use of force: Worden, 1995; Terrill and Mastrofski, 2002. Studies that have found that race does not influence the use of force: Reiss, 1968; Freidrich, 1980, Engel et al., 2000; Garner et al., 2002, Terrill, 2002.

satisfied with police service than white citizens (see Waddington et al., 2004; Dammer and Fairchild, 2006; Bowling et al., 2008; Miller, 2010). However, minority citizens are less likely to voice their dissatisfaction to officers in an encounter and instead are more likely to make a formal complaint later (Walters and Brown, 2000). This suggests that even when police encounters in the U.K. involve a minority citizen, those citizens are more likely to remain civil.

It was hypothesized that U.S. officers would be more likely than U.K. officers to anticipate and experience disrespect and it is argued here that this would hold true when looking only at white male officers in both countries. It can be asserted that variation in the amount of disrespect experienced could be the result of prejudice inherent in predominately white cultures, the social environment of policing dominated by white male officers, or the nature of police citizen encounters in both countries. Throughout time, the strained history of race relations has clearly crossed over to the police-citizen relationship.

In both countries, policing as an occupation has been and still is dominated by white male officers and given the authority afforded to police, race relations continue to be problematic. Skolnick (1966) discussed how an officer's 'working personality' led to the identification of 'symbolic assailants' which consequently led to alienation of police from the black community. While police officers may or may not display overt signs of prejudice, and while the behavior of black citizens may not be so different than the rest of the community, the racism inherent in a predominately white culture creates the police officer and the black citizen as a socially antagonistic pair (1966). Similarly, research in the U.K. has shown that officers still classify and stereotype citizens based on their ethnic origin (Bowling et al., 2008). These social perceptions and role orientations remain today and all else being equal, it can be asserted that white male police officers in both countries would perceive disrespectful behavior more often from black citizens.

The hypothesized difference then stems from the more general nature of situations in which police and citizens find themselves. In the U.S., black citizens may be unable or unwilling to consider an officer's point of view and that may lead them to act more assertively during encounters, in effect confronting and undermining the white officer's authority. In the U.K., minorities and resident-immigrants are less likely to behaviorally express such dissatisfaction during the encounter itself due to the fact that it violates the norms of acceptable behavior in the U.K. The cultural norms and expectations in the U.K. contribute to more congenial police-citizen encounters since both parties enter into encounters expecting that the other participant will act in an appropriate manner.

When discussing cultural norms, values, and homogeneity in the U.K., the recent influx of immigrants into the U.K. cannot be ignored. Now known as one of the most diverse cities in the world, London's foreign resident population has grown almost 800,000 in the past decade alone to approximately 2,288,000, almost 31% of London's population (Office of National Statistics, 2008).[22]

Keeping in mind the increases in residents, police officers, and PCSO's in London, the assertion could be made that London's racial and ethnic diversity could supersede traditional English communication norms and values. This assertion is less likely to be supported given that the country has made strong efforts toward inclusiveness. Referring to the entry of immigrants, Corner (2007:467) stated that England was more 'euro skeptic' in the 1960's but since the opening of its borders to the European Union, England sees itself as an 'EU in miniature' and seeks 'unity in diversity.'

This inclusiveness has translated to police as well. Even though the strong majority of officers are white, more minority officers and PCSO's are being hired and training has been modified to prepare them for the growing multi-racial and ethnic society that London has become (Metropolitan Police, 2007). In short, the MET has worked to train their officers to operate with cultural diversity issues in mind. So while minorities in both countries may find the police to be inherently prejudiced, what little literature there is still supports the notion that minorities will be less likely to behaviorally express any dissatisfaction with police at any time during the encounter (Walters and Brown, 2000). As such, white male officers in the U.S. will be more likely to experience disrespect than white male officers in the U.K.

Based on the above discussion, one hypothesis is generated:

---

[22] When the U.K. joined the European Union, the opening of their borders resulted in a record number of immigrants into the country and into London (Corner, 2007).

H$_9$: White male police officers in the U.S. will experience
disrespect more often than white male police officers in the
U.K.

Country Differences

In whatever country they occur, police-citizen encounters do not occur
in a vacuum. There are many internal factors that influence each
encounter but the limits of acceptable behavior can also be influenced
by outside sources as well. The norms and values of that country bring
in different sets of obligations and expectations. Moreover, a person's
country of residence (in relation to its norms) is one of the
circumstances that will influence his or her behavior in any given
situation. These normative expectations give rise to the boundaries of
allowable behaviors and can affect how officers perceive citizen
behaviors in police-citizen encounters.

Expectations of normative behavior may be no more evident than
in interactions where power imbalances exist. In both countries, the
imbalances are present in police-citizen encounters and as such,
officers' expectations of respect, deference, and compliance are
familiar to both officers and citizens. Simply put, a citizen's
compliance and respect are essential elements of these types of
encounters.

The divergence comes in relation to how officers define or
interpret certain citizen behaviors. Shared norms and customs,
especially in police-citizen encounters, give guidance to acceptable
behavior during interactions and imply that acceptable behaviors in one
country may be considered unacceptable or offensive in another. In
encounters where police are in the authoritative position and citizens
are expected to be subservient, the unwritten rules of acceptable
behavior play an important role and it must be recognized that these
rules may differ based on the police organization that officers are a part
of. Culture influences the norms of acceptable behavior and will have
an effect on the how a specific situation or encounter progresses and
although this research does not measure the effect of culture on
perceptions, it does take the normative behavioral expectations that
exist in each country into account. In short, this research examines
differences between police in two countries and attributes some of

those differences to unmeasured aspects of culture in these two countries (i.e. norms of communication) .

Anticipation and General Perception of Disrespect

Despite using the same language, these two countries are distinct. The U.K. is a historically homogeneous society and is one whose approach to interpersonal communications is known to be civilized and well mannered (see Waddington, 1999; Waddington, 1999a; Fox, 2005). Even as England and London have seen a steadily increasing foreign population with the opening of its borders to other European Union countries, they continue to be relatively homogenous with a strong sense of national identity.

While expectations of normative behavior are based on group consensus, shared values, and customs, they also require individuals to constrain or control their own actions through applying the consensus that's arisen. In the U.K., civility is an agreed upon component of their norms in relation to social interaction (see Fox, 2005) and it has even been asserted that faith in the police stems partly from the English identity and concept of social order in that country (Newburn, 2008). Furthermore, Jackson and Bradford (2009:511) stated that the police are seen as the "formal agent of social control" who are tasked with defending and restoring the "norms, values, and social cohesion of the community." This makes sense given that the formation of the police as an organization in the U.K. was more consensus-based rather than conflict-based (see Emsley, 2008). So when thinking about the importance of country differences, it is important to recognize that the police as an institution are there partly to maintain the concept of social order through the regulation of normative behavior, as well as legal statutes (see Moore, 2011).

This recognition is essential to understand since the norms of behavior in the U.K. do not change when a citizen confronts an authority figure. In fact, Jackson and Bradford (2009) found that U.K. citizens see the police as agents who promote social cohesion and behavioral norms leading to the implication that sets of behavioral norms cut across lines of authority. Hence, when confronting a police officer in the U.K., citizens in these encounters are expected to behave within the bounds of acceptability (see also Jackson and Sunshine, 2007). In the U.K., it is hypothesized that the shared norms related to social interaction allow citizens and officers to better understand the normative behavioral expectations of each other which could lead to less derisive police-citizen encounters. This in turn could lead to a reduced likelihood that citizens will act disrespectfully and that officers will perceive citizen disrespect less often. If officers perceive disrespect less often, then the likelihood of formal or informal sanctioning based on those behaviors should decrease.

In the historically diverse U.S., group consensus is not strong and there is not one dominant aspect to modes of acceptable communication. Indeed our country was founded upon the principle of individuality and is still considered to be a cultural melting pot, evidenced by our history of immigration and ever-increasing minority populations. Without this shared sense of norms and values, it becomes more difficult for citizens in police encounters to understand the boundaries of normative behavior and more importantly, to know which behaviors are going to be considered unacceptable by authority figures such as police officers. Without the strong sense of shared norms in the U.S. compared to the U.K., acceptable behavior by citizens in police encounters may become more difficult to identify by those citizens. Given this and the civil nature of interpersonal communications in the U.K., it would be reasonable to hypothesize that police officers in the U.K. would perceive that they encounter disrespectful behaviors less often than officers in the U.S.

This same influence would also have an effect on whether they anticipate disrespect prior to the encounter itself. It would be illogical to believe that officers in both countries enter into encounters without thinking about past experiences that they have had in similar situations. If officers in the U.K. expect civility more often and experience disrespect less often, it is reasonable to believe that they will have the tendency to enter into and define encounters as ones where disrespect is not anticipated.

Based on the above discussion, two hypotheses are generated:

H_{10}: Police officers in the U.K. will anticipate disrespect less often than police officers in the U.S.

H_{11}: Police officers in the U.K. will experience disrespect less often than police officers in the U.S.

Definitional Inclusivity

The civil nature of communication in the U.K. could also lead officers to formulate a definition of disrespect that is more inclusive than officers in the U.S. Having a definition that includes more behaviors does not necessarily imply that officers in the U.K. will experience disrespect more often than their U.S. counterparts. In fact, officers in the U.K. might find more behaviors to be disrespectful simply because they experience them less often. It stands to reason that if a specific behavior occurs on a rare basis, it is more likely to be noticed and acknowledged as non-normative. It follows that if officers in the U.K. anticipate that citizens will behave appropriately in encounters, then even minor transgressions might be considered disrespectful, precisely because they are rarer. For example, if citizens rarely use profanity in front of U.K. officers, then it stands to reason that an officer would be more likely to take note of that behavior and deem it to be disrespectful. Conversely, if cursing in front of officers in the U.S. occurs more regularly, those officers might be less likely to pay attention to a behavior that they see as the norm rather than the exception. In both cases, a particular citizen behavior may influence an officer's perception and have a stronger effect on an encounter outcome if it is one that officers rarely see.

Additionally, the Safer Neighbourhoods campaign (see Neyroud, 2009) and the Considerate Travel campaign (see Moore 2011) make clear that anti-social behavior (i.e. pushing, swearing, playing music loudly) is of primary concern to the British government and its enforcement agencies. The former focuses on anti-social behavior in neighborhoods and the latter focuses on behavior in the public transportation system but both campaigns seek to reduce the amount of anti-social behavior by citizens. It can be asserted that this emphasis only increases the probability that police officers in the U.K. will see and label these types of legal behaviors as disrespectful whereas U.S. officers may not.

Based on the above discussion, one hypothesis is generated:

H_{12}: Police officers in the U.K. will have a more inclusive definition of disrespect than police officers in the U.S.

Summary of Formal Hypotheses

People from various cultures maintain values, norms, and customs that inform them how to behave and how not to behave in social interactions and those behaviors could influence the how police-citizen interactions progress. These police-citizen encounters present clear power-imbalance and officers, will have certain expectations of appropriate conduct. When citizens step outside the boundaries of acceptable conduct, those behaviors may be deemed disrespectful by officers. The hypotheses justified above and summarized below make clear that factors related to the different countries and the different organizations can influence citizens' behaviors in encounters and officers' perceptions of those behaviors. In short, the historical, police role and function, officer, and country differences can influence how often officers anticipate and perceive disrespect in encounters with citizens, and how they define disrespect.

H_1: Armed police officers in the U.K. will be less likely to experience disrespect than unarmed police officers in the U.K.

H_2: Armed police officers in the U.K will be less likely to anticipate disrespect than unarmed police officers in the U.K.

H_3: In both countries, productive police officers will have a higher probability of experiencing disrespect than police officers who are less productive.

H_4: Productive police officers in the U.S. will have a higher probability of experiencing disrespect than productive police officers in the U.K.

H_5: In both countries, cynical police officers will experience more disrespect from citizens than police officers who less cynical.

H_6: In both countries, police officers who are older will experience disrespect less often than younger police officers.

H_7: In both countries, police officers who are more experienced will experience disrespect less often than less experienced police officers.

H_8: In both countries, more educated police officers will experience disrespect less often than less educated police officers.

H_9: White male police officers in the U.S. will experience disrespect more often than white male police officers in the U.K.

H_{10}: Police officers in the U.K. will anticipate disrespect less often than police officers in the U.S.

H_{11}: Police officers in the U.K. will have a more inclusive definition of disrespect than police officers in the U.S.

H_{12}: Police officers in the U.K. will experience disrespectful behavior less often than police officers in the U.S.

Chapter 4.

Tools and Procedures

Research Sites

The data for this research were collected in two city police departments in the spring of 2007: one in the U.S. and one in the U.K. For the purposes of this study, only those officers on regular patrol were surveyed. Officers on special assignment, investigators, and all supervisory personnel were deliberately excluded from this research. Given the primary goal of this research to understand how line officers on everyday patrol perceive citizen behavior, the inclusion of the other police personnel might confound the results.[23] Simply put, if sworn line officers are the ones encountering the public on a daily basis, then they should be the ones who will experience the most disrespect. As such, if a stronger understanding of citizen disrespect toward officers can be gained, those officers will be the ones who will benefit most from the results.

The first municipal department surveyed was a mid-sized city in the southeastern United States. Oak Ridge (pseudonym) has an estimated population of approximately 236,865 (U.S. Census Bureau, 2006). The City of Oak Ridge Police Department employs approximately 530 sworn personnel of which 400 are uniformed officers resulting in a 1:592 ratio of line officers to citizens. This is slightly lower than the 1:643 national ratio of line officers to citizens (U.S. Census Bureau, 2003; LEMAS, 2006).

---

[23] Future analyses should include these other groups for comparative purposes.

The London Metropolitan Police was the second police department used. London clearly has a much larger population than Oak Ridge[24] but the research in London will be limited to the three stations within the Royal Borough of Kensington and Chelsea (R.B.K.C.).[25] These three stations employ 556 sworn police officers (Blood, 2008). The 2001 population of the R.B.K.C. was 184,456 (Office of National Statistics, 2008),[26] much more akin to the population of Oak Ridge. That being said, the ratio of officers to citizens is 1:331, much lower than the ratio in Oak Ridge.

The MET is structurally and functionally similar to most larger municipal departments in the U.S., including Oak Ridge. They employ a para-military hierarchical structure and serve both crime control and service-based functions. Like departments in the U.S., the MET also divides responsibility into distinct patrol sectors and these sectors are set up to assure sufficient police coverage in each. The three stations in this sample have coverage responsibility for three specific areas within the R.B.K.C.: one affluent, one with residents that have varying incomes, and one that primarily includes a middle/lower middle class residential population.

Even though the populations within each sample jurisdiction are similar, two primary limitations exist when attempting comparison. First, the geographical area that the three borough stations cover is much smaller than the city of Oak Ridge. The R.B.K.C. covers 4.78 square miles to 116.6 square miles in Oak Ridge. The second and related limitation is that population densities are quite different. The R.B.K.C. has 38,589 citizens per square mile while Oak Ridge has 2,031 citizens per square mile (Office of National Statistics, 2008).

Sampling Design

A relatively small sample of 171 officers in two police departments was utilized for research and the study employed non-probability sampling methodology. These two particular departments were selected because

---

[24] The 2001 population of London was 7,172,091.

[25] The three stations were: Kensington, Chelsea, and Notting Hill.

[26] The Notting Hill Police station falls within the Royal Borough of Kensington and Chelsea.

both serve diverse populations, their police to citizen ratios were similar, and both were receptive to a research project of this kind. Even though both departments were receptive, they both placed restrictions on the project. Limitations were set by each department in relation to time, and access to officers and stations. Given this, purposive sampling was utilized as the sampling methodology for selecting both the departments and officers within each department. When studying a subset of a larger population, purposive sampling is appropriate when it would be nearly impossible to enumerate all of members of such population (here police departments in both countries). Additionally, purposive sampling is appropriate when comparing attributes or practices in different jurisdictions (Maxfield and Babbie, 2011). In this study, the question comes back to how similar sampled officers are to others not sampled in relation to their perceptions and experiences of disrespect.

With non-probability sampling, it is acknowledged that there is no way of estimating the probability that any one sampling element would be chosen for study. It would be similarly difficult to estimate any sampling biases that might result, and with this type of research, it would be very difficult to randomly sample departments in each country and officers within each department. Although sampling bias increases when using non-probability sampling methods, one cannot assume that the resultant sample will not be representative of the specific population.

As noted below in the procedures section, every officer from each department either coming onto shift (Oak Ridge) or entering the station canteen (London) was surveyed over a two or three day period. By distributing surveys to every officer, researcher bias in non-probability sampling can be mitigated. First, access to the officers within both departments was limited by the command staff. In Oak Ridge, there was no possible way to randomly sample officers coming onto shift given that the supervisors distributed the surveys and the researcher was only given access to the stations for retrieval of the surveys. The MET gave access to each station only for three consecutive days but that access was limited to the canteen/cafeteria. Given the time and access limitations set by each department, it would have been virtually impossible to randomly sample officers within the departments.[27] That being said, the distribution of surveys in each department yielded a sample that was surprisingly representative (see Table 5 and Table 8). Representativeness of the sample notwithstanding, the fact that the sample was obtained through non-probabilistic sampling methods is problematic and places limitations on the implications for interpretation. Purposive sampling limits the strength and efficacy of the findings. First, external validity is threatened. Without a truly representative sample, the ability to generalize the findings to other police departments (nationally and cross-nationally) is limited. Second, the non-representative nature of the sample places limits on what can be statistically accomplished and the results of the regression analyses must be taken with caution.

The data are also limited by the sample size. This research uses a relatively small sample of 171 officers (79 from Oak Ridge and 92 from London). This limited the scope of the analyses that could be conducted. For example, having the ability to separately analyze the influence of race and gender on the dependent variables would be valuable to the research. Unfortunately, the small number of black and female respondents made these analyses impossible. While these flaws are not fatal to the study, they must be acknowledged as problematic.

Table 5. Sample Representativeness*

	Oak Ridge Officers - Sample	Oak Ridge Officers - O.R.P.D.	London Officers - Sample	London Officers - R.B.K.C.
Race				
Black	13.9%	19.8%	6.5%	2.6%
White	82.4%	77.0%	90.2%	89.33%
Hispanic	2.6%	2.2%	0%	0%
Other			3.3%	8.6%

---

[27] Gaining permission to access police personnel and records can be difficult, especially when working to compare departments in two separate countries. Moreover, Bayley (1979) noted that police departments in the U.S. and in western Europe are noticeably more closed than departments in other parts of the world.

Table 5. (Continued) Sample Representativeness

	Oak Ridge Officers - Sample	Oak Ridge Officers - O.R.P.D.	London Officers - Sample	London Officers - R.B.K.C.
Gender				
Female	15.2%	15.3%	7.6%	22.6%
Male	83.5%	84.7%	92.4%	87.4%
Age	mean= 35.54	mean = 36.86	mean= 31.67	mean =35.92
Experience (in years)	mean= 11.46	mean =10.58	mean= 8.27	mean =10.33

*Oak Ridge does not compile information in relation to level of education. Neither the MET nor the R.B.K.C. were able to supply information in relation to level of education.

Participation and Refusal Rates

A total of 450 surveys were distributed; 200 in Oak Ridge and 250 in London. In Oak Ridge, surveys were distributed evenly in each of the department's four patrol sectors and given to supervisors for dissemination. In Oak Ridge, 79 officers returned completed surveys, yielding a response rate of 39.5%. In London, 92 (36.8%) of the 250 surveys were completed and returned. Direct approaches such as survey distributions typically yield lower return rates. Baruch (1999) argued that 20%-30% are typical return rates for organizations and when comparing responses rates in academic studies, she found that acceptable response for surveys of rank and file members of organizations should be in the range of 60% +/- 20%. The response rate in this research falls slightly below that benchmark but it is understandable given that the police are wary of completing even anonymous surveys from either inside or outside of the organization (see Adams 1995).

Procedures and Tools

Procedures

The following procedure was used in the administration and collection of the survey instrument. In Oak Ridge, the surveys were given to all officers coming onto shift over a two-day period by the shift supervisor. Each supervisor was given a form introducing the research to the officers. This form described the nature of the research and issues related to confidentiality, anonymity, and voluntary participation. Additionally, supervisors were instructed to tell officers not to complete the survey if they had already taken it in the past or if they had been interviewed on the same subject. Surveys (including an attached consent form) were distributed at that time and officers were asked to seal the completed survey in the provided envelope and to place the envelope into a sealed box. The boxes were then picked up by the researcher after the two-day period.

In London, the surveys were distributed over a three-day period in the station canteen/cafeteria where most officers met prior to each shift. Officers from Kensington and Chelsea utilized the Kensington canteen while Notting Hill officers had a canteen of their own. The researcher introduced the study utilizing the same form as was used in Oak Ridge. Anonymity, confidentiality, and voluntary participation were particularly stressed. Similar to Oak Ridge, completed surveys were returned in a sealed envelope and those envelopes were placed in a sealed box.

Survey Instruments[28]

Two virtually identical survey instruments were distributed to officers in both police departments (see Appendix A and Appendix B). The only differences were changes to sector/patrol area names, officer titles (police officer versus police constable), and offense names (i.e. driving under the influence versus drink drive). A detailed discussion of the survey questions relevant to the present hypotheses is discussed below. The survey instrument was adapted and modified from an interview instrument utilized by Pizio (2005). Pizio interviewed officers from the city of Oak Ridge in an effort to understand how they defined disrespect. This instrument was changed to reflect the change from an interview instrument to a survey instrument.

---

[28] Sound criticism exists for survey and interview research in that veracity of responses may be in question when admissions of impropriety are at stake (Maxfield and Babbie, 2011). Here, that might not be the case since this research only examined officers' perceptions of disrespect rather than any resultant conduct.

A pretest was conducted in the summer of 2006. The pretest revealed that the survey took approximately forty five minutes to complete and served to identify problems related to completion time and clarity of questions. As a result, several questions were either reworded or taken out and the completion time was reduced to approximately thirty minutes.[29]

The survey instruments were semi-structured and each consisted of twenty seven total questions. These included two open-ended questions, several close-ended questions, and questions related to attitude, productivity, and officers' demographics. The first question on the instrument asked officers how they would define or describe citizen disrespect. Officers were then asked to record as many disrespectful citizen behaviors as they could think of not knowing that a list of behaviors would be provided to them in later questions. The logic behind having officers answer these types of questions first stemmed from the need to obtain unguided and uninstructed responses rather than requiring officers to define disrespect based on the researcher's definition.

This second question relates directly to eleventh hypothesis and gave respondents the opportunity to respond the way they saw fit.[30] This maximized the opportunity to learn how officers interpret citizens' behaviors from their occupational viewpoint, an opportunity that would be limited by only asking more constrained close-ended questions. Based on the differing conclusions from past research, it was important to allow for responses that were not originally anticipated when the instrument was developed.

After these initial open ended questions, respondents were instructed to remove the last page of the survey, which contained a list

---

[29] A lengthy question was removed which asked respondents if they had anticipated or experienced disrespect from citizens with varying demographic characteristics including age, gender, race, and ethnicity. While these responses might have revealed valuable information, removal reduced completion time considerably. Research should address these citizen characteristics in the future.

[30] H_{11}: Police officers in the U.K. will have a more inclusive definition of disrespect than police officers in the U.S.

of both verbal and physical citizen behaviors (see Table 6).[31]   They were then asked which of these specific behaviors they deemed to be disrespectful. While the response frequencies could be inflated as a consequence of having a list in front of them, the value in providing a list of possible disrespectful behaviors allowed officers the opportunity to address behaviors that may not have occurred to them when answering the previous question. It is also important to note that the list of behaviors in Table 6 was formed by cross-referencing the indicators utilized in past research. This was in an effort to obtain a complete list of all possible disrespectful behaviors while avoiding overlap between such behaviors.

Table 6. List of Disrespectful Citizen Behaviors Provided to Officers

Verbal	Physical
Impolite or discourteous	Makes an obscene gesture
Verbally antagonistic	Spits toward/on officer
Ignores requests or commands	Takes a defensive/aggressive stance
Denies accusations	Physically resists arrest/detention
Curses/uses profanity	Physically assaults officer
Makes derogatory statement to officer	Attempts escape/flees on foot
Makes a physical threat to officer	Engages in a pursuit
Other verbally disrespectful behaviors	Other physically disrespectful behaviors

As Table 6 indicates, most of the verbal and physical behaviors are legally permissible while some are illegal. As Worden et al. (1996:328) noted: "... it would be a mistake to categorically exclude illegal acts from a conceptual definition of suspect demeanor instead of working to parse out the different effects of each." This same observation holds true for disrespect in that certain behaviors may be considered disrespectful by officers independent of their legality.

---

[31] These sixteen behaviors were chosen based on the fact that they have all been used in the various operationalizations of disrespect in past research.

Moreover, the behaviors include ones where the officer can make no judgments about a citizen's disposition. For example, an officer could believe that a citizen who flees on foot or in a vehicle may be acting disrespectfully without ever coming face-to-face with that citizen and without being able to determine that person's disposition. Additionally, an officer might find citizens disrespectful when they deny accusations, even when they do so in a polite fashion. The next set of questions sought to obtain information on how often they experienced disrespectful behaviors. Based on a four-point Likert scale[32], respondents were asked how often they experienced disrespect from suspects, arrestees, and victims in traffic encounters (DUI and non-DUI) , drug offenses, non-serious crimes, and serious crimes. Officers were also asked about their expectations of disrespect in encounters and which disrespectful behaviors they experienced more often in specific types of encounters. Officers were asked to indicate which behaviors were the most offensive to them personally and which disrespectful behaviors they experienced the most often. Later questions on the instrument focused on attitude, productivity, and demographics. Based on Likert scales, officers were asked questions on their distrust toward citizens and how their own number of arrests compared to others in their station.

The final set of questions sought demographic information. Officers indicated their race, gender, age, years of experience, level of educational attainment, and current patrol sector assignment. Comparing the responses of these questions to how often they experience disrespect will be the focus of the several hypotheses.

Operationalization of the Variables

This section includes the variable names, descriptions, and operationalizations.

Dependent Variables

Definition of Disrespect (DQsum, DSsum)

On the survey instrument, there were two questions that asked officers to list behaviors that they perceived as disrespectful. The first was an

---

[32] Responses: Often, sometimes, rarely, never, and no opinion.

open-ended question where they were asked to list all the disrespectful citizen behaviors they could think of. They were then given a list of disrespectful behaviors (see Table 6) and asked to indicate which of the listed behaviors they perceived to be disrespectful. For the eleventh hypothesis seeking which officers have a more inclusive definition of disrespect, analyses will be conducted on responses to the open-ended question first (DQsum) and then separate analyses will be conducted on the close-ended responses (DSsum).

These two dependent variables were constructed in the following manner. Distinct binary variables were created for each of the behaviors listed in Table 6 above. Behaviors that officers listed as disrespectful were quantified and coded as 1 (yes). If they did not list or mention the behavior, it was coded as 0 (no). For example, if an officer indicated that being verbally antagonistic was disrespectful, this was coded under the appropriate variable in the data file as a 1. If the officer did not indicate that s/he perceived this to be disrespectful, it was coded in the data file as a 0.

The benefit of this coding scheme is particularly important for the officers' qualitative responses since it allows for all behaviors to be taken into consideration instead of using ones that meet a certain threshold number of officers. Moreover, while the closed-ended question might over-inflate values (because officers were forced into categories), it might also be more reflective of their perceptions because they may have included specific disrespectful behaviors that they may have simply overlooked.

With both of these dependent variables, officers responded with other behaviors that were not included on the list provided to them. Two variables were formed based on officers' responses to the open-ended question. Between 10% and 20% of officers in both countries indicated that talking on a cell phone and making a racially derogatory remark were disrespectful to them. Given the frequency of these responses, the new variables were formed and were included in the analyses. Disrespectful behaviors that were listed only once by officers and that did not fit under any of the other variables were coded into two separate variables: other verbal and other physical (see Table 7). These two variables were included in the explanatory analyses.

Additionally, officers listed other behaviors that either did not occur in the officer's presence or were more general statements that did not imply a direct action by a citizen during or directly preceding a police encounter. These listed behaviors were not placed into any category and were excluded from analyses. These behaviors included: Failing to recognize police as an honorable profession, playing music too loud, criminal conduct outside of officer's presence (any crime, graffiti, littering), smoking indoors, and spreading rumors about police.

Table 7. Other Verbal and Physical Behaviors Listed by Officers

	Other Verbal	Other Physical
OAK RIDGE	Commands dog to attack, implying dishonesty, telling children not to talk to police, blaming officer for the law, dropping other officers' names	Urinating in front of officer, not standing still while stopped, any physical contact, damage to police buildings or equipment, throwing bodily fluid, littering in front of officer, not rolling down window when stopped, avoiding eye contact in encounters, touching police to get attention, defacing police car, failing to turn down music, rolling eyes, facing away during an interaction
LONDON	Laughing while stopped, talking in a foreign language, blame officer for not doing their job correctly, encouraging others to be disrespectful, inability to apologize	Eating while stopped, urinating in public, rolling eyes, physical contact, invasion of the officer's personal space, blowing smoke at officer, committing an offense in front of an officer, passing gas in front of officer, failing to turn down music, littering in presence of officer, laughing while in an encounter avoiding eye contact in encounters, sucking/kissing teeth

Once the data was coded, the individual behavior scores were altered in the following manner:

DQsum: In its original form, the data for this variable consisted of eighteen distinct binary behavioral indicators (see Table 6). Sixteen behaviors were on the original list and two were added during the coding process. 'Talking on the phone/cell phone during an encounter' and 'making a racially derogatory statement' were two responses that were not included on the original list of behaviors. These behaviors were listed by several officers.[33] Based on this, two new variables were created to reflect these responses.

Once coded, the data were then transformed into a variety score of disrespectful behaviors. This score took the binary indicators of disrespectful behaviors and simply summed them. This resulted in a single distinct continuous variable that represents the number of behaviors that officers believe to be disrespectful, with a range of possible values from 0-18. In histogram form, descriptive statistics for this variable are provided in Figure 1. As shown in Figure 1, most officers included 6-8 behaviors in their definition of disrespect.

Figure 1. Variety Score of Officer's Definition of Disrespect (Qualitative Responses)

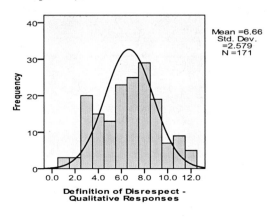

---

[33] Talking on the phone/cell phone during an encounter: n=17 (U.S. officers), n=10 (U.K. officers). Making a racially derogatory statement: n=19 (U.S. officers), n=9 (U.K. officers).

DSsum: This variable was constructed in much the same way as DQsum with one exception. One additional variable (making a racially derogatory remark) was constructed outside of the sixteen disrespectful behaviors from the list provided since it was the only behavior written in by more than one officer. This resulted in a single distinct continuous variable that represents the number of behaviors that officers believe to be disrespectful, with a range of possible values from 0-17. In histogram form, descriptive statistics for this variable are provided in Figure 2. When given the list of behaviors to choose from, the frequencies increased substantially with most officers including almost twice as many behaviors in their definition of disrespect.

Figure 2. Variety Score of Officer's Definition of Disrespect (Quantitative Responses)

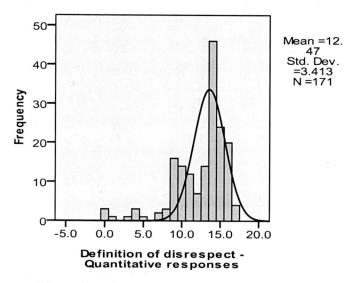

Perceived Disrespect (Dexperavg)

Of the twelve hypotheses presented in Chapter IV, perceived disrespect is the dependent variable in nine of them. Respondents were asked: How often have you <u>actually experienced</u> disrespect from citizens in these specific types of encounters? Officers responded with separate answers for each type of encounter listed and perceived disrespect in these individual types of encounters was measured ordinally based on four-point Likert scale.[34]   Encounters included: Domestic disputes, violent crime calls, non-serious crime calls, drug crime calls, drunk and disorderly calls, suspicious persons calls, calls for service/assistance, pursuits, traffic stops-DUI, traffic stops-non DUI.

Once coded, the data were then transformed into a score of encounters in which officers experienced disrespectful behaviors. This score was the result of taking the sum of the ordinal indicators and averaging them.   This resulted in a single continuous variable that represents how often officers perceived that they had experienced disrespectful behaviors in different types of encounters, with a range of possible values from 1-4.   It is this continuous variable of perceived disrespect that will be used in the regression analyses. In histogram form, descriptive statistics for this variable are provided in Figure 3.

Figure 3. Officer's Perception of Experiencing Disrespect

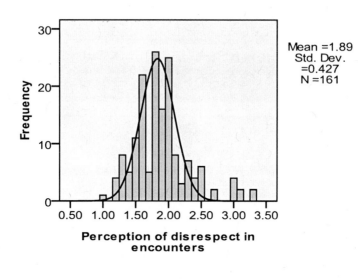

Mean =1.89
Std. Dev.
=0.427
N =161

[34] Responses: Always, sometimes, rarely, never.

Anticipated Disrespect (antidich)

Officers were asked: In your experience as a police officer, have you ever received a _____ call *where* (prior to arrival), you anticipated that you would encounter a disrespectful citizen? Officers responded with separate answers for each type of encounter listed above.[35] Initially, these ten encounter-based variables were measured dichotomously (1= anticipated disrespect prior to arrival, 0= did not anticipate disrespect prior to arrival) but were then summed to form a single variety score of anticipated disrespect (see Figure 4).

The resulting distribution was skewed heavily to the left with approximately 33% of all officers anticipating disrespect in all encounter types. As a result, the variable was recoded in a single dichotomous variable (1=anticipated disrespect in all encounter types, 0=anticipated disrespect in less than all encounter types). It is this variable that was utilized in the logistic regressions (see Figure 5).

Figure 4. Officer's Anticipation of Disrespect (summed variety score)

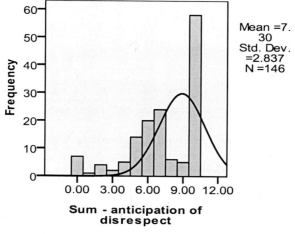

---

[35] Encounters included: Domestic disputes, violent crime calls, non-serious crime calls, drug crime calls, drunk and disorderly calls, suspicious persons calls, calls for service/assistance, pursuits, traffic stops-DUI, traffic stops-non DUI.

Figure 5. Officer's Anticipation of Disrespect (dichotomous)

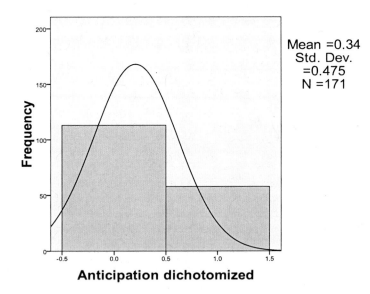

Independent Variables[36]

Demographic Characteristics

Demographic characteristics relevant to this research are age, race, gender, and educational attainment. As independent variables, they were measured in the following manner. Age (age) was measured in years as a continuous level variable. Due to the low number of females and blacks in the sample, only white males from both countries will be compared. Based on this, a nominal level dummy variable for race/gender was created with the following coding scheme: 1= white males, 0=all others in sample.[37] This variable was then recoded and all

---

[36] See Table 8 for descriptive information on the independent variables.

[37] The hypotheses that examine differences between productive officers (H_4) and white male officers in each country (H_9) will utilize an interaction term. Utilizing interaction terms are useful when the analysis seeks to understand a relationship between two variables beyond the linear or additive effects. Instead, analyses using interaction terms seek to "specify the conditions

those in the sample that were not white males were designated as missing and not included on the analysis. Educational attainment (educ) was measured as an interval level variable. Respondents were asked how many years of education they had completed. The following coding scheme was utilized: 1= high school diploma, 2= < 2 years college, 3= < 4 years college, 4= 4 or > years college.

Job-Related Characteristics

Job-related characteristics relevant to this research are experience, current assignment (vehicle or foot patrol), firearms, productivity, and cynicism. As independent variables, they were measured in the following manner. In relation to experience (totalyrs), respondents were asked to indicate how many years they had been a police officer allowing for open ended responses. As such, experience was measured in years as a continuous level variable.

Since all officers in the sample were on regular patrol, the question on the survey instrument asked what their current mode of patrol was (assign). In the U.K., officers were asked if they were on foot patrol, vehicle patrol, or firearms vehicle patrol. For U.S. officers in the sample, all were on vehicle patrol and all carried firearms. As a result, current assignment for U.K. officers was measured nominally and utilized the following coding scheme: 1= foot patrol, 2 = vehicle patrol, 3= vehicle patrol with firearms.

Whether or not officers carried a firearm was also relevant to this research but the data only permit comparing armed and unarmed officers in London. In Oak Ridge, all officers carried firearms and will be excluded from this portion of the research. In London, only specially trained officers are authorized to carry a firearm on regular patrol. On the London instrument, this information was obtained from the survey question asking about their current assignment (see above). This variable (for London officers) was recoded into a new variable that

---

under which a causal relationship is weakened (moderated) or strengthened (amplified)" (Aiken and West, 1991: .2). In other words, the value of the dependent variable may jointly depend on the value of two predictor variables. In this research, it is predicted that experiencing disrespect may depend jointly on the country in which the officers work and certain officer-specific characteristics (productivity and white/male).

combined foot and vehicle patrol into one attribute and vehicle patrol with firearms as the other attribute (armed). This variable was measured ordinally and utilized the following coding scheme: 0= unarmed, 1= armed.

The productivity variable (arrcomp) was based on officers' self reports of how many arrests they make compared to other officers in their station. This variable was measured ordinally on a five-point Likert scale and used the following coding scheme: 1= substantially more arrests, 2= more arrests, 3= about the same amount of arrests, 4= less arrests, 5= substantially less arrests.

Cynicism (dstrust2) was also measured ordinally. In an effort to reveal the level of cynicism, subjects were asked whether or not police officers have a reason to be distrustful of most citizens. A five-point Likert scale was used for the possible responses. Thus, this variable was measured ordinally and utilized the following coding scheme: 1= agree strongly, 2= agree somewhat, 3= no opinion, 4= disagree somewhat, 5= disagree strongly.

Table 8. Sample Characteristics

Demographic Characteristics	Oak Ridge Officers N=79	London Officers N=92
Age	mean= 35.54 s.d.= 8.98	mean= 31.67 s.d.= 6.15
Race		
Black [0]	11 (13.9%)	6 (6.5%)
White [1]	65 (82.4%)	83 (90.2%)
Hispanic [2]	2 (2.6%)	0
Gender		
Female [0]	12 (15.2%)	7 (7.6%)
Male [1]	66 (83.5%)	85 (92.4%)

Table 8. (Continued) Sample Characteristics

Education[38]	Oak Ridge Officers N=79	London Officers N=92
	mean= 2.99 s.d.= 1.23	mean= 2.24 s.d.= 1.18
Job related Characteristics		
Total Experience (in years)	mean= 11.46 s.d.= 8.72	mean= 8.27 s.d.= 5.85
Firearms		
Armed [1]	79	12
Unarmed [2]	0	79
Productivity		
Substantially more arrests [1]	3 (3.9%)	3 (3.6%)
More arrests [2]	5 (6.3%)	15 (18.1%)
About the same amount of arrests [3]	44 (57.1%)	42 (50.6%)
Less arrests [4]	14 (18.2%)	7 (8.4%)
Substantially less arrests [5]	11 (14.3%)	16 (19.3%)
Cynicism		
Agree strongly [1]	10 (12.7%)	14 (16.3%)
Agree somewhat [2]	34 (43.0%)	21 (24.4%)
No opinion [3]	16 (20.3%)	16 (18.6%)
Disagree somewhat [4]	17 (21.5%)	33 (38.4%)
Disagree strongly [5]	2 (2.5%)	2 (2.3%)

---

[38] The attributes for level of education included: High school [1]; < 2 yrs college/university [2]; < 4 yrs college/university [3]; =/> 4 yrs college/university [4].

Analytic Strategy

Descriptive Statistics

First, descriptive analyses were conducted to compare officers' responses and to reveal differences between officers in each country. This included an examination of anticipation, and the prevalence of experiencing disrespectful citizens both generally and in specific types of encounters. Additionally, descriptives are given outlining the behaviors officers find to be the most offensive.

Due to the small sample size and the non-random nature of the sample, chi square analyses are performed and two measures of association will be utilized in ascertaining any differences between anticipation/experience and the two countries. For anticipation of disrespect phi (Φ) was used and the effect sizes are noted. Phi is an appropriate measure of association when the two variables in the equation are nominal level variables and are dichotomous (see Champion and Hartley 2010). For the descriptive analyses related to how often officer experience disrespect in encounters and with different categories of citizens, Cramer's V was used and the effect sizes are noted. Cramer's V is an appropriate measure of association with ordinal level variables and has no sample size restrictions (Champion and Hartley 2010).

Effect size is a name given to a family of measures that assess the magnitude of a treatment effect where significance tests would be inappropriate. Unlike significance tests, these measures are independent of sample size and make them appropriate for use in this research (Cohen, 1988). The effect sizes for the descriptive models are determined following the guidelines set forth by Rea and Parker (1992): "weak to moderate $\geq.20$ and $<.40$," "moderate$<.60$," and "strong<1.0."

Inclusivity of Definition (DQsum + DSsum) (H11)

The inclusivity hypothesis works to determine which group of officers has a more inclusive definition of disrespect. Put differently, which country's officers have a definition of disrespect that includes more behavioral indicators? It is hypothesized that officers in the U.K. will have a broader definition of disrespect.

As noted above, the open-ended responses from the first question on the instrument were quantified into individual dichotomous variables. Once quantified, a new variable (DQsum) was created that summed the individual scores and resulted in a single continuous variable for analysis. This same recoding process was conducted for the close-ended question (DSsum) asking officers which behaviors they deemed to be disrespectful from the list provided. The descriptive analysis revealed that the mean inclusivity for U.S. officers was greater than for U.K. officers (DQsum). While simple comparison on its own would be valuable, it is important to account for other variables that might influence the means. For example, the mean level of experience was higher for officers in the U.S. It is possible that these officers may have had more opportunity to be exposed to disrespectful behaviors which may in turn influence which behaviors they include in their definition. In short, it is important to understand to what degree of difference in means is due to factors other than the country in which the officers work.

As such, ordinary least squares regression (OLS) was conducted to determine if a difference exists while controlling for other factors that might influence inclusivity. This same procedure was then completed for close-ended question (DSsum) in an effort to validate the open-ended one (DQsum). The frequency distributions for the quantitative definition of disrespect (DSsum) for officers in both countries revealed outliers which skewed the distribution to the left (see Figure 3). As a sensitivity test, analyses that include this dependent variable will be re-run excluding the outliers.

In addition to the aggregate models described above, categorized models (verbal disrespect and physical disrespect) were analyzed via OLS and behavior-specific models were analyzed via a linear probability model. While the aggregate models can reveal the breadth of officer's definition of disrespect, it would be interesting to determine if they are responding differentially to any specific items. Moreover, a possibility exists that the results will reveal no significant differences in overall inclusiveness, the interpretation being that there is no difference in the sum of behaviors that officers in both countries find to be disrespectful. However, officers in each country might endorse different specific behaviors even though they endorse the same number of behaviors on average.

For example, officers in the U.K. might find more verbal behaviors to be disrespectful than their counterparts in the U.S. It could be expected that the majority of officers in both countries would find spitting or assault to be disrespectful but as the behaviors become less egregious (i.e. impoliteness, swearing), the possibility exists that the differences between countries would become more accentuated. Differences may even exist between verbal and physical disrespect. Categorizing behaviors and then examining individual behaviors could reveal important patterns in how officers see and perceive disrespect. As such, OLS will be used on the categorized models and a series of linear probability models will be regressed on the behavior-specific models.

When assessing the results of the regression equations here, effect sizes will be utilized to assess the presence and strength of the relationships between the relevant independent variables in each model and the respective dependent variable(s). The sample for this study is non-random and was obtained through non-probabilistic methods. Moreover, the sample size is relatively small. Given these two characteristics of the sample, the use of statistical significance to assess the models would be improper.

The effect size for each model will be obtained by dividing the standardized regression coefficient by the standard deviation of the respective dependent variable. The magnitude of the individual effect size for each equation will be "small $\geq$ .2," "medium $\geq$ .5," and "large $\geq$ .8". While the assignment of effect sizes are arbitrary, they are used in many empirical studies (see Cohen, 1988).

Anticipation of Disrespect (antidich) (H2, H10)

These hypotheses were analyzed utilizing two separate models to determine if officers' levels of anticipating disrespect vary based on the country they work in or the fact that they are armed. A logistic regression was used to estimate the effect of these two independent variables on the variety score of anticipation.

While logistic regression was used as the primary model, it is important to be attentive to the distributional form of the dependent variables. Here, anticipation is measured as a dichotomous. A Poisson model was used to validate the results from the logistic regression for the anticipation hypotheses. This type of analysis can serve as a sensitivity test to ensure that the results of the logistic regression are robust. If differences exist between the two regression coefficients, then the more appropriate model is the Poisson due to the fact that it takes into account how the dependent variable is measured and distributed.

Perception of Disrespect (experavg) (H1, H3-H9, H12)

The remaining nine hypotheses were analyzed utilizing OLS. The models sought to estimate the impact or effect of the key independent variables on the mean score of perceived disrespect to ascertain whether certain characteristics of officers in each country influence their perceptions that they have experienced disrespect. Since the race/gender and productivity hypotheses compare the effect of these two characteristics across countries, an interaction term was formed and was included in those specific models. Similar to the definitional inclusivity analyses, the use of effect sizes will be used to assess the presence and magnitude of the relationships between perception of disrespect and the independent variables in each individual model.

Chapter 5
Results – Descriptive Statistics

Introduction

In most explanatory research, descriptive statistics set the stage for the multivariate analysis to follow. Prior to any substantive comparisons, it is important to gain an initial understanding of what kinds of behaviors actually occur in police-citizen interactions. More specifically, the descriptive statistics in this research help tell the story of what behaviors officers are encountering, the specific types of encounters that those behaviors are occurring in, and to what extent they are occurring. This information can give officers the opportunity to make predictions of what they may encounter prior to entering into a specific type of interaction and at a very basic level, affords officers the ability to create and apply operational strategies to prevent disrespect and react appropriately when they encounter it.

Do officers anticipate disrespect before entering encounters? If so, are there specific types of encounters where disrespect is anticipated more than others? Once they enter into encounters, does their anticipation become reality? When they do encounter disrespect, which specific behaviors are occurring more often? It is important to understand the answers to these questions because any pre-encounter anticipation could influence behaviors and outcomes in encounters. Furthermore, knowing which behaviors are more prevalent in a given type of encounter could guide training and officers could be prepared to prevent any escalation of the encounter once disrespect occurs.

Additionally, the differences between officers in each country is of central importance to this analysis and even given the small sample size, the information presented here can begin to shed light on how disrespect is perceived by officers in the U.S. and the U.K. Moreover, these results will reveal differences between officers in the two countries that are useful without further analysis. For example, results related to the more common and more egregious affronts in each country can reveal which behaviors are more problematic for officers in each department. Additionally, understanding which behaviors occur in specific types of encounters can also be valuable, as noted above. While the question of whether cultural differences influence behaviors in encounters cannot be answered in this chapter, the descriptive statistics can reveal information that the multivariate analyses can take further.

Thinking about police encounters chronologically, this chapter will proceed in the following manner. First, descriptives will be reported detailing how often officers anticipate disrespect prior to entering into specific types of encounters. The prevalence of disrespectful behaviors during the course of specific encounter types will then be examined followed by a breakdown of disrespect in encounters by citizen role (suspect, arrestee, and crime victim). With an understanding of the prevalence of disrespect, attention will then turn to the most common disrespectful behaviors that officers encounter and ones that officers in both countries found to be most offensive. The chapter will end with an examination and comparison of how officers in each department define disrespect.

On a final note, there is a limitation with the data presented below. While most U.S. officers responded to most questions, more U.K. officers left questions blank and this yielded a higher amount of missing information for those officers. The results presented below are the valid frequency percentages. In other words, the percentages are based on the officers that did respond to each specific question on the survey instrument.

Anticipation of Disrespect

Prior to the discussion detailing the extent to which officers perceive disrespect from citizens, officers' expectations prior to encounters must be considered. Officers were asked if they entered into encounters anticipating that they would experience disrespect. Although one would hope that any anticipation on an officer's part would not influence their experiences, this possibility cannot be ignored. If an officer enters into an encounter expecting disrespect, the possibility exists that their behavior might become more authoritative leading to a disrespectful response from citizens. While this analysis will not discover the relationship between anticipation and experience, it is still important to understand if officers enter into encounters anticipating disrespect from citizens and is an appropriate starting point for the analysis.

Table 9. Percentage of Officers that Anticipated Disrespect in Specific Encounters(a)[39]

		Percent of Officers that Anticipated Disrespect	
Domestic	**U.S. N= 75**	82.7	χ^2=.61
Disputes	**U.K. N= 71**	87.3	Φ = .065
Serious Crime	**U.S. N= 73**	76.7	χ^2=8.80
	U.K. N= 70	94.3	Φ = . 248*
Non-serious	**U.S. N= 71**	47.9	χ^2=008
Crime	**U.K. N= 70**	47.1	Φ = -.007
Drug Offenses	**U.S. N= 75**	77.3	χ^2=6.77
	U.K. N=70	92.9	Φ = .216*
Drunk +	**U.S. N= 75**	85.3	χ^2=8.36
Disorderly	**U.K. N= 70**	98.6	Φ = .240*
Suspicious	**U.S. N= 73**	57.5	χ^2=5.04
Persons	**U.K. N= 69**	75.4	Φ = .18
Service Calls	**U.S. N= 72**	41.7	χ^2=16.44
	U.K. N= 69	75.4	Φ = .341*
Pursuits	**U.S. N= 72**	79.2	χ^2=.12
	U.K. N= 70	81.4	Φ = .028
DUI Violations	**U.S. N= 75**	80.0	χ^2=1.34
	U.K. N= 70	87.1	Φ = .096
Traffic	**U.S. N= 73**	65.8	χ^2=1.96
Violations	**U.K. N= 70**	54.3	Φ = .117

a. df = 1 for all analyses.
b. Effect size denoted as: *es≥.20 and <.40, **es<.60, ***es<1.0.

As noted in Chapter 4, effect sizes are commonly used to assess relationships when the data does not allow for traditional tests of statistical significance. To determine the magnitude of the relationship between country and anticipation in the respective encounter types, phi was computed and the effect sizes are noted. Phi is appropriate when measuring the associations between dichotomous variables (here anticipation and country) and values of phi can range from -1 to 1 and values closer -1 or 1 indicate stronger relationships between the two variables (see Rea and Parker, 1992).

When examining the data in this table, several patterns emerge. First, it is clear that officers in both countries think about the possibility of disrespect and that they do anticipate disrespect prior to entering into encounters. Table 9 reveals that officers in both countries anticipate disrespect in all encounter types. Additionally, more officers in both countries expected that they would experience disrespect in encounters where the citizen was intoxicated or posed a threat to the officer or public. As this table shows, officers in both countries had higher rates of anticipation in DUI's, serious crime calls, domestic disputes, drug offenses, drunk and disorderly calls, and pursuits. Given the unpredictability in these types of encounters, this result was not unexpected. U.K. officers reported low levels of anticipation with non-serious crime calls while U.S. officers had low levels of anticipation with service calls.

Second, officers in the U.K. had higher levels of anticipation in serious crime calls, drug calls, drunk and disorderly calls, suspicious persons calls, and service calls. They also had an overall higher average percentage of encounters where they anticipated disrespect. These higher levels of anticipation in the U.K. could be due to the fact that the U.K. has a much lower violent crime rate than that in the U.S. Accordingly, they may be more unfamiliar with these types of encounters and it is reasonable to expect a heightened sense of uncertainty and anticipation any time an officer goes into a type of encounter that they are rarely called to.

Third, even though officers had high rates of anticipation, some encounter types showed marked differences between officers in the two countries. The differences were especially large in those encounter types where danger or citizen sobriety were in question. This is not wholly unexpected given the unpredictable nature of these types of calls but officers in the U.K. anticipated disrespect at a much higher rate in serious crimes, drunk and disorderly and drug offenses. In fact, U.K. officers reported that they anticipated disrespect in almost all drunk and disorderly calls that they are sent to (98.6%).

One other result that is worthy of mention is that 75% of U.K. officers anticipated disrespect in service calls compared to only 41% of U.S. officers. This could be due to the fact that many U.K. officers are on foot patrol and unarmed. These officers may be more likely to be called to service-related events or they may simply define service calls different than U.S. officers.[40] Moreover, the U.K. sample was with London based officers and given the multicultural and multi-national nature of London's resident and visitor populations, service calls might not run as smoothly as in the U.S. Without more information, it would be difficult to parse out the reasons for their anticipation of disrespect in service calls.

When examining these results as a whole, it is clear that officers anticipate disrespect in encounters and more officers indicated that they expected disrespect in the types of encounters that were more unpredictable. Generally, U.S. officers anticipated disrespect less often than U.K. officers and those officers in the U.K. anticipated disrespect in more encounter types. These differences were particularly notable with encounters where the citizens may be intoxicated or where the encounter is dangerous and unpredictable.

Experience - Specific Types of Encounters

The results related to anticipation revealed that officers anticipate disrespect and that their anticipation varies by encounter type. Additionally, more officers in the U.K. anticipated disrespect in many

---

[40] There is anecdotal evidence to suggest that the latter assertion is correct. In response to this unexpected result, five MET officers were informally interviewed in March 2009. Officers were randomly approached while they were either on foot patrol or in a vehicle in London. When asked how they would define 'service call,' none of the five knew or understood what a service call was. Once explained, they indicated that their equivalent to service calls (non-law enforcement related calls) would be labeled as 'civil disputes' and that they experienced disrespect in those types of calls. None of the officers knew of any label or category that would encompass non-law enforcement related calls that did not involve disputes.

encounter types. These results run contrary to what was hypothesized and bring up the possibility that U.K. officers' experiences might be consistent with their levels of anticipation. Using a four-point Likert scale, officers responded to a series of survey questions which asked how often they had experienced disrespect in the same specific encounters noted above.

Similar to the descriptive analyses related to anticipation, effect sizes were also used when assessing the relationships between encounter and citizen types, and officers' perceptions of disrespect. In these analyses, however, Cramer's V was computed to determine the magnitude of the relationships. Cramer's V was utilized since the perception of disrespect is an ordinal variable (see Champion and Hartley, 2010). With Cramer's V, values closer to 1 indicate a stronger relationship between the variables (see Rea and Parker, 1992).

Table 10a. Prevalence of Disrespect in Specific Types of Encounters (in percentages)

		Often	Some-times	Rarely	Never	
Domestic	**U.S. N= 79**	73.4	25.3	1.3	0.0	χ^2=13.61
Disputes(a)	**U.K. N= 80**	46.7	44.4	8.9	0.0	V=.293*
Serious	**U.S. N= 73**	50.7	38.4	11.0	0.0	χ^2=.737
Crime(b)	**U.K. N= 82**	55.3	34.1	10.6	0.0	V=.069
Non-serious	**U.S. N= 79**	8.9	65.8	25.3	0.0	χ^2=4.05
Crime(c)	**U.K. N= 82**	4.3	66.0	27.7	2.1	V=.159
Drug	**U.S. N= 79**	45.6	54.4	0.0	0.0	χ^2=8.72
Offenses(d)	**U.K. N= 82**	51.1	40.4	6.4	2.1	V=.233*
Drunk +	**U.S. N= 79**	73.4	21.5	5.1	0.0	χ^2=4.26
Disorderly(e)	**U.K. N= 82**	70.2	29.8	0.0	0.0	V=.163
Suspicious	**U.S. N= 79**	6.3	70.9	22.8	0.0	χ^2=3.46
Persons(f)	**U.K. N= 82**	12.8	68.1	19.1	0.0	V=.147
Service Calls	**U.S. N= 79**	2.5	44.3	53.2	0.0	χ^2=16.73
(g)	**U.K. N= 82**	21.3	29.8	46.8	2.1	V=.322*
Pursuits(h)	**U.S. N= 73**	49.3	34.2	13.7	2.7	χ^2=9.60
	U.K. N= 82	34.0	48.9	17.1	0.0	V=.249*

Table 10a. (Continued) Prevalence of Disrespect in Specific Types of Encounters (in percentages)

		Often	Some-times	Rarely	Never	
DUI	U.S. N= 77	32.5	62.3	5.2	0.0	χ^2=12.66
Violations(i)	U.K. N= 82	21.3	53.2	25.5	0.0	V=.282*
Traffic	U.S. N= 77	10.4	64.9	24.7	0.0	χ^2=3.52
Violations(j)	U.K. N= 82	12.8	74.5	12.8	0.0	V=.149

a. $df = 2$.
b. $df = 2$.
c. $df = 3$.
d. $df = 3$.
e. $df = 2$.
f. $df = 2$.
g. $df = 3$.
h. $df = 3$.
i. $df = 2$.
j. $df = 2$.
k. Effect size denoted as: *es$\geq$.20 and <.40, **es<.60, ***es<1.0.

Based on Table 10a, experiencing disrespect 'often' in the U.S. is more prevalent in encounters typically associated with either an intoxicated citizen or where a citizen is putting another in danger. More officers experienced disrespect 'often' in domestic disputes, serious crime calls, drug offenses, drunk and disorderly calls, pursuits, and DUI's. Domestic disputes and drunk/disorderly calls had much higher percentages than the others in this category and this was not unexpected. Interestingly, the exception to this trend was with DUI violations. Only 32.5% of officers in the U.S. indicated that they experienced disrespect 'often' in DUI encounters compared to the 62.3% of officers who experienced disrespect 'sometimes.' Non-serious crime, suspicious persons calls, service calls and traffic stops all had a substantially lower percentage of U.S. officers indicating that they experienced disrespect 'often' in these types of encounters.

In the U.K., this same pattern was present but less pronounced. U.K. officers were more likely to experience disrespect 'sometimes' in most of the different encounter types (except domestics, serious crimes, drug offenses, and drunk/disorderly calls) but not as likely to experience disrespect 'often.' U.K. officers also reported substantially higher percentages of drunk/disorderly calls where they experienced disrespect 'often' but like U.S. officers, the prevalence of disrespect was lower in DUI encounters.

When comparing the two groups of officers, it becomes clear that they both experience disrespect in encounters that are traditionally more unpredictable or dangerous. Drunk and disorderly calls rank highest among all encounter types and given that these encounters bring in both levels of sobriety and the possibility of an altercation, this result is not unexpected. It is also interesting to note that a much higher percentage of U.S. officers indicated that they experienced disrespect in domestic disputes, pursuits, and DUI's compared to U.K. officers implying that there may be higher levels of civility in these types of encounters in the U.K.

Table 10b. **Prevalence (collapsed) of Disrespect in Specific Types of Encounters (in percentages)**

		Often/Sometimes	Rarely/ Never
Domestic Disputes	U.S.	98.7	1.3
	U.K.	95.0	5.0
Serious Crime	U.S.	89.1	11.0
	U.K.	91.4	8.5
Non-serious Crime	U.S.	74.7	25.3
	U.K.	71.9	28.0
Drug Offenses	U.S.	100.0	0.0
	U.K.	93.9	6.1
Drunk + Disorderly	U.S.	94.9	5.1
	U.K.	100.0	0.0
Suspicious Persons	U.S.	77.2	22.8
	U.K.	87.8	12.2
Service Calls	U.S.	46.8	53.2
	U.K.	48.8	51.2
Pursuits	U.S.	83.5	16.5
	U.K.	69.3	20.6
DUI Violations	U.S.	94.8	5.2
	U.K.	74.3	25.6
Traffic Violations	U.S.	75.3	24.7
	U.K.	86.6	13.4

When using the four-point Likert scale, the responses from officers give a clear picture of how often they are experiencing disrespect in the specific encounter types. Using the four-point scale, the general trends may be less transparent. While both tables reveal meaningful information, the two-point Likert scale may give a better sense of the prevalence of disrespect. When the scale was collapsed into a two-category scale (see Table 10b), it becomes clear that disrespect is much more common in most offense types. In fact, officers in both countries reported high percentages in all encounter types except service calls. When comparing the two countries, the pattern of U.S. officers experiencing disrespect more often than U.K. officers weakened with the exception of DUI's and pursuits. In these encounters, U.S. officers experienced disrespectful citizens much more often than officers in the U.K.

Two other noteworthy pieces of information come out of the above tables. First, officers in both countries indicated that they experienced disrespect often/sometimes in nearly all domestics, drug offenses, and drunk/disorderly encounters. Disrespectful citizens in these types of encounters are clearly more problematic for officers than in other types of encounters, as evidenced by both the high levels of anticipation and actual experiences. Second, officers in the U.K. encountered disrespect 'often' in 22% of service calls compared to only 2.5% of officers in the U.S. This is similar to the results in Table 9c where U.K. officers anticipated disrespect at a much higher rate at service calls compared to U.S. officers and could be due to how officers in the U.K. define 'service call.'

While it is gratifying to see that disrespect occurs rarely in some encounters, it is unfortunate that officers in both countries have experienced some type of disrespect in the majority of encounter types. In very few cases did officers from either country indicate that they had never experienced disrespect in the different encounter types. This trend persisted when officers were asked to break down their experiences with disrespect by encounter type and role of citizen (see Tables 11a-11c).

Tables 10a and 10b reveal that officers in both countries experience disrespect in all encounter types and officers in the U.K. experienced disrespect 'often' in more encounters types. Some pronounced differences were also found. For example, disrespect in domestic disputes was much more common in the U.S. and disrespect at service calls was much more common in the U.K. In Table 10b, the two-point scale mitigated many of these differences and officers in both countries experienced disrespect at more similar rates.

Overall, the above descriptive statistics revealed mixed results. In some encounter types, U.S. officers experienced more disrespect and in others, U.K. officers saw more disrespect. In both countries, however, it is clear that disrespect occurs more often in encounters where sobriety or danger to the officer or public is in question. At this point, it is important to note that the above questions asked officers about the prevalence of disrespect at encounters without regard to the role of the citizen in those encounters. To further understand the complexity of disrespect in encounters, it is also important to dissect the relationship between disrespect and the role of the citizen in select encounters.

Experience - Role of Citizen

As seen in Tables 11a, 12a, and 13a, U.K. officers experienced disrespect 'often' more than U.S. officers in all encounter categories and across the different types of citizens.[41] In many of these encounter types, the differences were substantial. When the Likert scale was collapsed into two categories (see Tables 11b, 12b, and 13b), U.S. officers experienced more disrespect in all encounter types except for non-serious crime victims and traffic arrestees (those who were cited for a traffic violation). It was hypothesized that U.K. officers would experience disrespect less often than U.S. officers and even though U.K. officers experienced disrespect 'often' from suspects at a higher rate than U.S. officers, the results reported in Tables 11b, 12b, and 13b seem to work toward supporting that hypothesis.

It was striking to find that U.K. officers experienced disrespect 'often' with traffic suspects at a rate almost six times that of U.S. officers. While this difference narrowed once traffic suspects were arrested/cited, it remained the biggest difference across all encounter

---

[41] It should be reiterated that the percentages reported are from those officers who responded to the specific question. This is especially relevant with U.K. officers since not all are assigned to vehicle patrol. Those officers would not engage in any traffic stops, DUI stops, or pursuits.

types and citizens, over twice as much. This raises an important question although it is one that cannot be answered by this specific research endeavor; Why do traffic stops in the U.K. yield so much more disrespect, from both suspects and those ticketed? It is also interesting to note that disrespect generally does not decrease once suspects become arrestees. U.K. officers still experience disrespect 'often' more than U.S. officers but other than a slight decrease in disrespect at U.K. traffic stops and with serious crime arrestees in the U.S., disrespect remained prevalent. One other notable finding pertains to non-serious U.K. crime. Tables 11a and 11b reveal that once U.K. officers arrest suspects of non-serious crime, their experiences with disrespect 'often' increase substantially.

Once the results were collapsed into a two-point scale, it becomes clear that U.S. officers experience disrespect more often than U.K. officers. In every category save for traffic suspects and non-serious crime victims, U.S. officers reported higher percentages of perceived disrespect. Equally important, the percentages in Tables 11a-b and 12a-b also confirm that officers in both countries experience high rates of disrespect from the suspects and arrestees that they encounter.

Table 11a. Prevalence of Disrespect in Encounters with Suspects (in percentages)

		Often	Some-times	Rarely	Never	
Traffic Stops(a)	U.S. N= 79	6.5	79.2	14.3	0.0	χ^2=29.67
	U.K. N= 80	36.2	48.8	8.8	6.2	V=.432*
DUI (b)	U.S. N= 79	37.7	54.5	7.8	0.0	χ^2=13.94
	U.K. N= 80	38.5	37.2	20.5	3.8	V=.296
Non-serious Crime(c)	U.S. N= 79	13.9	73.4	12.7	0.0	χ^2=10.22
	U.K. N= 80	22.1	54.5	20.8	2.6	V=.254*
Serious Crime (d)	U.S. N= 79	32.9	50.6	11.4	5.1	χ^2=15.43
	U.K. N= 80	42.9	26.0	27.3	3.9	V=.312*

a. *df* = 4.
b. *df* = 5.
c. *df* = 4.
d. *df* = 5.
e. Effect size denoted as: *es≥.20 and <.40, **es<.60, ***es<1.0.

Table 11b. Prevalence (collapsed) of Disrespect in Encounters with Suspects (in percentages)

		Often/Sometimes	Rarely/Never
Traffic Stops	U.S.	85.7	14.3
	U.K.	85.0	15.0
DUI	U.S.	92.2	7.8
	U.K.	75.7	24.3
Non-serious	U.S.	87.3	12.7
Crime	U.K.	76.6	23.4
Serious Crime	U.S.	83.5	16.5
	U.K.	68.8	31.2

Table 12a. Prevalence of Disrespect in Encounters with Arrestees (in percentages)

		Often	Some-times	Rarely	Never	
Traffic	U.S. N= 79	14.3	72.7	13.0	0.0	χ^2=26.95
Stops(a)	U.K. N= 79	36.5	51.4	8.1	0.0	V=.413*
						*
DUI (b)	U.S. N= 79	37.7	58.4	3.9	0.0	χ^2=15.36
	U.K. N= 79	40.5	44.6	6.8	8.1	V=.312*
Non-	U.S. N= 79	19.0	70.9	10.1	0.0	χ^2=18.03
serious	U.K. N= 79	45.9	45.9	8.2	0.0	V=.338*
Crime (c)						
Serious	U.S. N= 77	27.3	53.2	14.3	5.2	χ^2=7.77
Crime(d)	U.K. N= 79	38.2	36.8	21.1	3.9	V=.223*

a. $df = 5$.
b. $df = 5$.
c. $df = 3$.
d. $df = 5$.
e. Effect size denoted as: *es$\geq$.20 and <.40, **es<.60, ***es<1.0.

Table 12b. Prevalence (collapsed) of Disrespect in Encounters with Arrestees (in percentages)

		Often/Sometimes	Rarely/Never
Traffic Stops	U.S.	87.0	13.0
	U.K.	91.9	8.1
DUI	U.S.	96.1	3.9
	U.K.	85.1	14.9
Non-serious Crime	U.S.	89.9	10.1
	U.K.	81.9	8.1
Serious Crime	U.S.	80.5	19.5
	U.K.	75.0	25.0

While it is important to understand how often police officers are experiencing disrespect from those subject to police power, the survey also asked officers to assess the extent of disrespect from crime victims. This examination of officers' experiences with crime victims (Tables 13a-b) tells the same story. While officers in both countries experience disrespect less often from victims than suspects and arrestees, they still experience it at a rate higher than one would expect. For example, officers in the U.K. experienced disrespect often/sometimes with 42.9% of their non-serious crime victims. It would be reasonable to assume that disrespect would be less prevalent from victims and while these results confirm that, the rates are still higher than one would anticipate given that officers are present to assist rather than arrest.

Table 13a. Prevalence of Disrespect in Encounters with Crime Victims (in percentages)

		Often	Some times	Rarely	Never	
Non-serious Crime(a)	U.S. N= 75	6.7	29.3	52.0	12.0	χ^2=13.58
	U.K. N= 77	10.3	42.6	36.8	10.3	V=.354*
Serious Crime(b)	U.S. N= 75	4.0	37.3	46.7	12.0	χ^2=19.03
	U.K. N= 77	12.3	21.5	50.8	15.4	V=.299*

a. df = 5.
b. df = 5.
c. Effect size denoted as: *es≥.20 and <.40, **es<.60, ***es<1.0.

Table 13b. Prevalence (collapsed) of Disrespect in Encounters with Crime Victims (in percentages)

		Non-serious Crime	Serious Crime
Often/Sometimes	**U.S.**	36.0	41.3
	U.K.	52.9	33.8
Rarely/Never	**U.S.**	64.0	68.7
	U.K.	47.1	66.2

    The results above show that U.K. officers experience disrespect 'often' at a rate higher than U.S. officers but when collapsed into a two-point scale, the results confirm the earlier results and it becomes clear that U.S. officers experience more disrespect than U.K. officers. While unfortunate, it is important to note that officers in both countries reported experiencing high rates of disrespect across all encounter types from both suspects and arrestees. While it is less likely for officers to experience disrespect from crime victims, the results from Tables 13a and 13b make clear that disrespect is not limited to those who are at odds with police or who are subject to arrest from them.

Experience - Most Common Displays of Disrespect

While the results presented above describe officers' experiences, they do not shed light on which behaviors are more common in specific types of encounters. Given that most police encounters progress without incident and that police use of physical force occurs at very low rates (see Adams, 1999; Garner et al., 2002), it is reasonable to expect that officers will encounter verbally disrespectful behaviors more than physical ones and that the verbal disrespect will be at the lower end of the seriousness spectrum. For example, many involuntary police encounters do not end in arrest or citation for the citizen. As such, one would expect impoliteness or antagonism to occur at higher rates than derogatory statements made about the officer or verbal threats made to the officer.

    So when working to understand which disrespectful behaviors occur more often in specific encounter types, it is important to step back for a moment to consider the impact that this information could have. If officers are going to experience disrespect in encounters, knowing which behaviors are more common can have clear implications for training. If officers can enter into encounters with an idea of what type of disrespect they are likely to encounter, they can also be ready to deflect or de-escalate that disrespect prior to or once it occurs.

As expected, officers in both countries experienced disrespect at the lower end of the spectrum more often than serious or physical displays of disrespect (see Table 14a). In both countries, verbal disrespect was much more prevalent than physical disrespect by a wide margin (see Table 14b). Given the low percentage of encounters where any use of physical force occurs both toward and by officers, it is understandable how citizens might not act in a physically aggressive manner that officers would deem disrespectful.

As seen in Tables 14a and 14b below, verbal disrespect is more common in all but one encounter type. Only during pursuits did officers in both countries find physical disrespect to be the most common form of disrespect they encountered. U.S. officers indicated that citizens physically resist arrest and officers in the U.K. responded that 'ignoring commands' and 'taking a defensive stance' were the most common behaviors in their pursuits. The 'ignoring commands' response by U.K. officers could be a result of the citizen failing to stop their vehicle when officers activate their emergency lights and siren. In all other encounters, verbal displays of disrespect were much more common than physical displays.

It is interesting to note that officers in the U.K. indicated that impoliteness was the most common form of disrespect in all but two encounter types. U.S. officers on the other hand, responded with a wider range of verbal behaviors that they encountered more often. It is also noteworthy that in three encounter types (DUI, traffic, and drug offenses) , U.S. officers responded that they experienced citizens who denied accusations as the most common form of disrespect.

Table 14a. Most Common Displays of Disrespect in Specific Encounter Types

	U.S.	U.K.
Domestic Disputes	Impolite	Impolite
Serious Crime	Verbally antagonistic + Ignores commands	Impolite
Non-serious Crime	Impolite	Impolite

Table 14a. (Continued) Most Common Displays of Disrespect in Specific Encounter Types

	U.S.	U.K.
Drug Offenses	Denies accusations	Impolite
Drunk + Disorderly	Curses	Denies accusations + Curses
Suspicious Persons	Impolite	Impolite
Service Calls	Impolite	Impolite
Pursuits	Physically resists	Ignores commands + Takes defensive stance
DUI Violations	Denies accusations	Impolite
Traffic Violations	Denies accusations	Impolite

Table 14b. Most Common Displays of Disrespect in Specific Encounter Types: Verbal vs. Physical Displays of Disrespect

	U.S.		U.K.	
	Verbal	Physical	Verbal	Physical
Domestic Disputes	97.4	2.6	92.5	3.7
Serious Crime	72.6	27.4	84.8	15.2
Non-serious Crime	90.7	9.3	92.5	7.5
Drug Offenses	72.0	28.0	89.5	10.5
Drunk + Disorderly	82.6	17.4	80.8	19.2
Suspicious Persons	97.3	2.7	82.3	17.7
Service Calls	100.0	0.0	71.0	29.0
Pursuits	46.6	53.4	43.6	56.4
DUI Violations	92.0	8.0	84.8	15.2
Traffic Violations	94.6	5.4	100.0	0.0

While it is logical to assume that verbal disrespect would be more common than physical disrespect, and while Table 14a supported this assertion, it is still important to gain a clearer picture as to the degree of the difference. When grouping the disrespectful behaviors into verbal and physical disrespect categories, the relationship holds. In all but the pursuit category, verbal disrespect is much more common in both countries.

It is reasonable to assume that pursuits would yield a higher rate of physical disrespect since offenders have made clear that they are seeking to elude capture. If offenders are willing to evade police in vehicles, then the expectation of physical confrontation upon the termination of a pursuit is not an unreasonable one. That being said, the substantially higher percentage of physical disrespect in pursuit-related encounters could also be explained by officers being physically aggressive upon termination of pursuits.

Apart from pursuit, Table 14b revealed that U.K. officers experienced a substantially higher rate of physical disrespect in service calls. U.K. officers indicated that in service calls where disrespect occurred, physical disrespect occurred in 29.0% compared to no incidences of physical disrespect in the U.S. A closer examination revealed that the most prevalent disrespectful behaviors in service calls in the U.K. were pursuit, making an obscene gesture, assault, and spitting. Given the non-law enforcement nature of service calls compared to encounters related to criminal violations, it seems unlikely that this physical disrespect would be that prevalent. In addition, since pursuit was the most prevalent disrespectful behavior in service calls, it is possible that that these officers may have a different definition of 'service call' than officers in the U.S., as noted earlier.

Based on the overall results put forth in Tables 14a and 14b, it is apparent that verbal disrespect is much more common than physical disrespect and that minor affronts are more common to U.K. officers than their U.S. counterparts. Moreover, compared to the variety of verbally disrespectful behaviors that U.S. officers encounter, impoliteness is a behavior that U.K. officers encounter on a more consistent basis across most encounters types. The descriptive information presented above begins to illustrate what officers are encountering in the field and how often they're experiencing it but it is also important to understand if officers deem some disrespectful behaviors to be more offensive than others.

Experience - Most Offensive Displays of Disrespect

If future research will seek to understand how officers react to disrespectful behaviors, it is important to understand which behaviors officers find to be more egregious than others. Officers might be more inclined to formally or informally sanction those citizens who exhibit behaviors they find to be the most serious affronts in addition to the initial reason the encounter was occurring in the first place. Practically, the same assertion can be made as was made above. If officers understand which behaviors they deem to be more disrespectful, they can enter into encounters with increased levels of awareness and can hopefully sanction based on the criminal actions rather than any disrespectful behaviors exhibited.

In relation to disrespectful behaviors officers found to be most offensive, there were mixed results. Not surprisingly, spitting and assaulting an officer were considered to be the most egregious by the majority of officers in both countries. In contrast, U.K. officers found a wider range of behaviors to be affronts that they were most offended by. Only five behaviors received no responses (compared to ten for U.S. officers), and verbally disrespectful behaviors accounted for over 30% of what U.K. officers found to be most offensive. U.S. officers indicated that there were a variety of other verbal displays of disrespect that were most offensive including dropping names, implying the officer is dishonest, talking on a cell phone, and telling their kids not to talk to police.

Table 15. Most Offensive Display of Disrespect (in percentages)

	U.S.	U.K.
Impolite or discourteous	0.0	4.3
Verbally antagonistic	0.0	4.3
Argues or denies accusations	6.6	6.5
Curses/uses profanity	2.6	2.2
Makes derogatory statement to officer	0.0	4.3
Makes a physical threat to officer	0.0	4.3
Other verbal	18.4	4.3
Makes an obscene gesture	0.0	0.0

Table 15. (Continued) Most Offensive Display of Disrespect (in percentages)

	U.S.	U.K.
Takes a defensive/aggressive stance	0.0	0.0
Spits toward/on officer	51.3	43.5
Attempts escape/flees on foot	0.0	0.0
Engages in a pursuit	0.0	0.0
Physically resists arrest/detention	0.0	0.0
Physically assaults officer	21.1	23.9
Other physical	0.0	2.2

Definitional Inclusivity

When examining citizens' behaviors that officers believe to be disrespectful, the data suggests that officers in both countries have consistent views as to the types of behaviors they include. Overall, when first asked to describe citizen disrespect without a list in front of them, officers' answers included all of the behaviors listed on the researcher-generated list along with two additional categories (talking on a cell phone and making a racially derogatory statement). Since the list was developed from past conceptualizations, it implies that past research has not been off target in their efforts to define disrespect for study. The difference lies in the fact that while past studies have included many of these behaviors, they have not been utilized as a group in any single study. Moreover, the results indicated that officers had a wide range of behaviors that they considered to be disrespectful including behaviors unrelated to a citizen's attitude or temperament toward the officer, such as talking on a cell phone and attempting escape/fleeing.

Oak Ridge

Prior to being provided the list, more officers in Oak Ridge found low level verbal behaviors to be disrespectful than physical ones. Impoliteness, ignoring requests, and cursing were the top responses. These findings are not surprising since these behaviors were ones which officers encountered more often (see Table 14a). Surprisingly, only 59.5% indicated that spitting toward/on them was disrespectful and only 58.2% indicated that assault on an officer was disrespectful.

As noted above, two behaviors were added to this list once the responses were coded. Making a racially derogatory statement and talking on a cell phone during a police encounter were deemed disrespectful by 24.1% and 21.5% of officers, respectively. These were the only two behaviors that have not been specifically utilized in past conceptualizations but that were deemed disrespectful by more than one officer.

Table 16. Behaviors that Oak Ridge Officers Deemed to be Disrespectful[42]

Citizen Behaviors	% officers deeming behavior to be disrespect - uninstructed	% officers deeming behavior to be disrespect - from provided list
Impolite or discourteous	72.2	88.3
Ignores requests or commands (a)	72.2	97.4
Curses/uses profanity	69.6	84.4
Spits toward/on officer	59.5	100
Verbally antagonistic (b)	59.5	94.8
Physically assaults officer	58.2	100
Denies accusations	53.2	76.6
Makes derogatory statement (c)	45.6	97.4
Makes an obscene gesture	31.6	92.2
Makes a racially derogatory statement (d)	24.1	32.9
Takes defensive/aggressive stance	24.1	97.4
Physically resists arrest/detention	22.8	87
Talking on a cell phone (e)	21.5	
Makes a physical threat to officer	20.3	100

---

[42] Only responses from two or more officers were included in Tables 16 and 17. Although excluded, these responses can be viewed in Chapter V, Table 7. While not included here, they were included in the causal analysis as 'other verbal' or 'other physical.'

Table 16. (Continued) Behaviors that Oak Ridge Officers Deemed to be Disrespectful

Citizen Behaviors	% officers deeming behavior to be disrespect - uninstructed	% officers deeming behavior to be disrespect - from provided list
Attempts escape/flees on foot	11.4	77.9
Engages in a pursuit	5.1	76.6
Average	39.4	86.9
Range	67.1	67.1

(a) This category was collapsed and included: noncompliance, not following orders or commands (to move), being completely quiet, and giving no relevant information when asked.

(b) This category was collapsed and included: verbal antagonism, antagonistic, verbal abuse, verbal hostility, outwardly hostile, and belligerent.

(c) This category was collapsed and included: derogatory statements made toward the police, the officer, or their family.

(d) Officers added this behavior when responding to both questions (uninstructed and when provided the list of behaviors).

(e) No officer added this behavior when provided with the list of behaviors.

After Oak Ridge officers responded to the open-ended question, they were given a list of behaviors and were asked to indicate which of these behaviors were disrespectful. With these responses, almost all of the frequencies increased substantially. This was expected and was a result of being given specific choices to respond to. The only behavior which did not increase substantially was making a racially derogatory statement (8.8% increase) but this was due to the fact that it was not on the initial list[43] and officers wrote in this response in an open space on the questionnaire. Interestingly, all Oak Ridge officers indicated that spitting, assault on an officer, and making a physical threat toward an

---

[43] Making a derogatory comment was included on the list but making a 'racially' derogatory comment was not.

officer were disrespectful. Moreover, over 75% of officers indicated that every behavior provided on the list was disrespectful.

From these results, it's clear that Oak Ridge officers include more behaviors in their definition of disrespect than has been used in past research. When answering without the list in front of them, officers' responses indicated that the more common the behavior is, the more likely it is to be included in their definition (i.e. impoliteness, ignoring commands, cursing). After officers were given the list, the behaviors they included in their uninstructed responses stayed the same, however, the behaviors that more officers found to be disrespectful moved from low level verbal behaviors (i.e. impoliteness, ignores command) to physical and threatening behaviors (i.e. assault, spitting, making threats). Additionally, spitting, assault, and physical threats were found to be disrespectful by all officers and other than making a racially derogatory statement, more than 75% of all officers agreed that all of the behaviors were disrespectful toward them.

London

In London, the results were very similar to those of U.S. officers (see Table 17). Overall, the same behaviors were included in the responses from officers in both countries but slightly fewer U.K. officers found these behaviors to be disrespectful. Interestingly, the top five behaviors chosen by U.S. officers were exactly the same as the choices as U.K. officers. Additionally, spitting toward/on an officer was the behavior found disrespectful by most officers but after that, four of the top five behaviors were all low level verbal behaviors. The results also revealed that despite its illegality, less than half of the officers stated that assaulting a police officer was disrespectful.

When U.K. officers were provided the list of behaviors, the frequencies increased, again substantially. Similar to officers in the U.S., spitting and assault were the behaviors with the highest frequency. After spitting and assault, the next six behaviors were all forms of verbal disrespect with at least 75% of officers stating that the behaviors were disrespectful to them. Consistent with the cultural rationales set forth in Chapter IV and officers' responses indicating that it was the most common form of disrespect they encountered (see Table 14a), 94.4% indicated that impoliteness was disrespectful. Only spitting and assault had higher frequencies.

Table 17. **Behaviors that London Officers Deemed to be Disrespectful**

Citizen Behaviors	% officers deeming behavior to be disrespect - uninstructed	% officers deeming behavior to be disrespect - from provided list
Spits toward/on officer	66.3	96.7
Curses/uses profanity	64.1	75.6
Verbally antagonistic (a)	63.0	87.8
Impolite or discourteous	53.3	94.4
Ignores requests or commands (b)	51.1	88.9
Physically assaults officer	44.6	96.7
Denies accusations	37.0	70
Makes derogatory statement (c)	31.5	91.1
Makes an obscene gesture	29.3	92.2
Makes a physical threat to officer	18.5	91.1
Attempts escape/flees on foot	14.1	68.9
Takes defensive/aggressive stance	14.1	61.1
Talking in a cell phone (d)	10.9	
Makes a racially derogatory statement (e)	9.1	28.3
Physically resists arrest/detention	8.7	72.2
Engages in a pursuit	2.2	34.4
Average	32.4	76.6
Range	64.1	68.4

(a) This category was collapsed and included: verbal antagonism, antagonistic, verbal abusive, confrontational, verbal hostility, and belligerent.

(b) This category was collapsed and included: noncompliance, not following orders or commands (to move), being completely quiet, not obeying, and giving no relevant information when asked.

(c) This category was collapsed and included: derogatory statements made toward the police, the officer, or their family.

(d) No officer added this behavior when provided with the list of behaviors.

(e) Officers added this behavior when responding to both questions (uninstructed and when provided the list of behaviors).

Definitional Inclusivity Comparison

When comparing the responses of officers in both countries, several patterns emerged. First, when asked to describe or define disrespect prior to seeing any list, all of their initial responses centered on the obvious: specific and overt citizen behaviors in face-to-face encounters (see Tables 16 and 17). The responses of more officers focused on low level verbally disrespectful behaviors and apart from spitting toward/on an officer, the top five responses were impoliteness, verbal antagonism, curses/uses profanity, and ignores requests or commands. Based upon the frequency of these responses and the fact that these were the first responses from every officer, it is apparent that when thinking about personal affronts, officers paid much more attention to these behaviors during encounters than anything else. This result was expected given that these behaviors are ones that officers experienced more often (more generally and in different encounter types - see Table 14a).

When comparing the two countries, it is interesting to note the similarities with officers' qualitative responses. First, while frequency ordering differences existed, the list of behaviors that officers found to be disrespectful were identical. Moreover, they were the same behaviors that have been utilized in various conceptualizations in past studies. The only exceptions to this are two behaviors that have not been utilized as distinct attributes of disrespect in past studies and that were not part of the list provided to officers in a later question. Officers in both countries found making a racially derogatory remark (24.1% in the U.S. and 9.1% in the U.K.) and talking on a cell phone (21.5% in the U.S. and 10.9% in the U.K.) to be disrespectful.

Second, the order in which officers believed behaviors were disrespectful was more alike than different. As noted above, the top five behaviors were the same for officers in both countries. When looking at the remainder of the behaviors, there are discrepancies in the exact ordering but those differences are minor. They indicate that officers in both countries have very similar views as to which behaviors they deem to be disrespectful. When examining the prevalence of their responses, the lists also indicate how disrespectful officers find these behaviors to be.

With two exceptions, these patterns also held true when examining the behaviors that officers found to be disrespectful once a list was provided to them. First, the frequencies for most of the behaviors increased substantially for the reasons noted above. Second, the ordering of the behaviors was different than officers' qualitative responses with physical behaviors (i.e. spitting, assault) increasing in frequency more than other behaviors. Given these changes and increases in frequencies, it is interesting to note that the changes in ordering were also consistent among officers from the two countries. Spitting and assault on an officer became the response that more officers deemed disrespectful and this was not unexpected given that officers in both countries believed these behaviors to the most egregious (see Table 15). Even with this difference, when examining the overall frequencies and ordering in Tables 16 and 17, it is clear that officers in both countries have similar views as to what they deem to be disrespectful and that a single definition of disrespect can be utilized for study in both countries.

An Officer-based Definition of Disrespect

Understanding what officers deem to be disrespectful is the first step toward empirically determining if discretionary responses occur as a result of such disrespect. As this research demonstrates, officers in the U.S. characterize disrespect in a manner that is more inclusive than prior conceptualizations. Moreover, officers in the U.K. have almost identical views as to how they characterize disrespectful behaviors. Although Klinger (1994) and Worden et al. (1996) brought this definitional concern to light, it's been thirteen years since research has devoted itself to advancing a more concise and valid definition of citizen disrespect. With this in mind, Table 18 outlines the resulting officer-based definition of disrespect for officers in both countries.

This definition differs from others presented in the body of literature as a whole in two distinct ways; there is an increased inclusiveness of disrespectful behaviors and disrespect is not limited to hostile or antagonistic behaviors. First, U.S. officers were more inclusive in their definition of disrespect than in past studies and included behaviors that ranged from minor verbal affronts to considerably more serious physical affronts such as physical attacks or spitting on an officer.[44] Additionally, no two studies have utilized the

---

[44] Given the small sample size, the behaviors listed in Table 18 may not comprise all of the behaviors that officers believe to be disrespectful. While the results here indicate a more inclusive definition of disrespect than seen in past research, collecting data from a larger sample could reveal different

same conceptual definition and as such, this definition of disrespect gives future research the opportunity to consistently utilize a conceptualization formed by officers allowing for a more comparable body of research.

Table 18. Behaviors Forming an Officer-Based Definition of Disrespect*

Citizen Behavior	Operational Definition
Impolite or discourteous to officer	Citizen is impolite and it is directed toward/at officer
Verbally antagonistic	Citizen is verbally hostile, belligerent, abusive, or overtly rude
Ignores requests or commands	Citizen is noncompliant, does not follow orders or commands (to move), is completely quiet when asked to respond, or gives no relevant information when asked
Curses/uses profanity	Citizen uses profanity in the officer's presence
Makes a derogatory statement	Citizen makes derogatory statement directed toward the officer or their family
Makes a racially derogatory statement	Citizen makes derogatory statement directed toward the officer in relation to the officer's race
Denies accusations	Citizen denies accusation/wrongdoing for an offense committed in the presence of the officer or for an offense where evidence of guilt is clear to officer
Makes a physical threat to officer	Citizen makes a direct physical threat to officer

categories or could elevate the single response categories listed in Table 7 into more meaningful categories.

Table 18. (Continued) Behaviors Forming an Officer-Based
Definition of Disrespect*

Citizen Behavior	Operational Definition
Talks on a cell phone	Citizen converses on a cell phone when the officer is speaking directly to the citizen
Makes an obscene gesture	Citizen makes an obscene gesture toward officer
Takes a defensive/ aggressive stance	Citizen takes an aggressive or fighting stance
Spits toward/on officer	Citizen spits on officer or spits in officer's general direction
Attempts escape/flees on foot	Citizen flees from officer on foot prior to or after arrest/detention
Engages in a pursuit	Citizen flees from officer in a vehicle
Physically resists arrest/detention	Citizen physically resists officer's attempt to arrest/detain
Physically assaults officer	Citizen physically assaults officer with hands, feet, or weapon

* Note: behaviors ordered from verbal to physical.

It was interesting to find that officers in the U.K. held similar characterizations of disrespect. Outside of the responses from only one officer that were placed into the 'other' category, the only marked difference was the frequency of their responses to the open-ended question. The behaviors they included were identical to those of U.S. officers and even included talking on a cell phone and making a racially derogatory remark, neither of which have been used in any prior conceptualization. This held true for the quantitative responses as well.

It was surprising to find these similarities given the cultural differences between these two countries and these results tend to support the assertion regarding the similarity of officers in different parts of the world (see Westmarland 2008). So even if the characteristics of a country's culture influence citizens' behaviors (which the multivariate analyses address), culture may not have as strong an effect on officers' outlooks and perceptions in relation to citizen disrespect. As such, officers in both countries have strikingly similar views as to what behaviors they deem to be disrespectful. There is a second way in which this definition differs from past conceptualizations. Officers in both countries reported that disrespectful behaviors included ones that were not verbally hostile or antagonistic. These behaviors fall into two categories; one which includes behaviors that occur prior to the face-to-face encounter and the other which includes behaviors that occur during the encounter itself.

In the first category, officers indicated that they find it disrespectful when a citizen flees or engages the officer in a vehicle pursuit (see Tables 16 and 17). Unlike Reisig et al. (2004) who adopted a definition of disrespect which excluded all physical acts, officers here indicated that disrespect can include physical acts that occur prior to any face-to-face contact. With these behaviors (pursuit, flees on foot), officers are unable to make judgments or interpretations of citizen's disposition or attitude. As such, future conceptualizations should move away from a more limited one that includes only verbal behaviors or ones that only allow for an assessment of the citizen's attitude.[45]

The second category includes non-hostile or antagonistic citizen behaviors during the face-to-face interaction between officers and citizens. For example, officers in both countries believed that denying accusations and talking on a cell phone during an encounter were disrespectful. Past conceptualizations fall short by constraining their definitions by only including citizen behaviors that are antagonistic toward the officer (in face to face encounters), suggesting that conceptualizations must be inclusive or they risk underestimating the effect of disrespect on police decision making.

Additionally, responses from officers in both countries supported Worden's et al. (1996:327) assertion that we should not "assume that affronts of varying gravity are all equivalent in officers' eyes." For example, officers explicitly asserted that certain behaviors such as spitting or assault were more serious affronts than others. Police seek

---

[45] It must be noted that a smaller percentage of officers believed these to be disrespectful when answering the open-ended question but these percentages increased as the others did when responding to the close-ended question and allow for inclusion in the definition.

compliance with their commands and when they tell citizens how to behave, it is expressed in the context of their broad, generally defined legal authority (see Mastrofski et al., 1996). When a citizen's behavior becomes disrespectful, it is reasonable to suggest that disrespect of different magnitudes (and unrelated to criminal conduct) could exist and that officers would believe that not all legally permissible and illegal affronts are equal in their eyes. Parsing out the effects of legal and illegal forms of disrespect is crucial for future causal research but for the purposes of this research, it is important to understand that officers in both countries include both forms of disrespect in their definition.

Chapter Summary

The descriptive statistics reported above give insight to officers' experiences with disrespect. In both countries, officers reported that they perceive verbal disrespect more often than physical disrespect and that even within the larger category of verbal disrespect, most of the reported behaviors were at the low end of the spectrum (i.e. impoliteness). While conclusions regarding any differences between the countries should be taken with caution, the descriptive analysis did reveal patterns implying differences between officers in each country.

When disrespect was broken down by encounter type, the results were mixed. Officers from both countries were more likely to experience disrespect in encounters where danger existed or where sobriety was at issue. This trend was clear in the U.S. but was less pronounced with officers from the U.K. When encounters were further broken down and examined based on the role of the citizen (suspect, arrestee, victim), U.S. officers were more likely to experience disrespect, consistent with what was hypothesized. Conversely, U.K. officers were more likely to anticipate disrespect in most encounter types, contrary to what was hypothesized.

In relation to definitional inclusivity, the results were much more consistent. Officers in both countries had similar views as to which behaviors they included in their definition of disrespect and the resulting definition can be applied to research in both countries. Moreover, the resulting definition was more inclusive than in past research and did include both legal and illegal behaviors.

Officers in both countries are by no means untouched by disrespectful citizens and the above results shed light on their experiences. These descriptive statistics are the first step toward understanding more about officers' experiences with disrespect and how officers define disrespect. When considering the individual countries or when making preliminary comparisons, the patterns that have emerged give insight into whether or not officers anticipate disrespect, what disrespectful behaviors they experience, and how often those disrespectful behaviors occur. The following chapter will take the next step of comparison by testing the effects of various factors that influence officers' experiences with disrespect via multivariate regressions.

Chapter 6.

Anticipation of Disrespect and Definitional Inclusivity

Introduction

In the next two chapters, the results of the multivariate analyses are reported. This chapter begins with a preliminary assessment of the relationship between the relevant variables and will be reported in the form of a bivariate correlation matrix. This is followed by the multivariate analyses for the hypotheses related to anticipation and definitional inclusivity. The results related to the two anticipation hypotheses are reported first. Definitional inclusivity results are reported and include the findings of the aggregate model, disrespect broken down into verbal and physical behaviors, and behavior-specific models. The results concerning the hypotheses related to perception/experience are reported in the next chapter.

Logistic regression was utilized for the anticipation analyses and ordinary least squares regression was utilized for the definitional inclusivity analyses. In any form, multivariate regression allows one to estimate the relationship between the primary independent variable(s) while controlling for other factors that may also have an influence on the dependent variable(s). By controlling for these variables, one can reduce the probability that any predicted relationships are spurious. Gender, race, education, and experience were controlled for in each of the regression equations.

As noted above, this first multivariate results chapter assesses the hypotheses related to definitional inclusivity and anticipation while the second multivariate results chapter tests all of the hypotheses related to officers' perceptions. By changing the order in which the analyses are presented, it allows for all of the perception-based hypotheses to be tested in the same chapter resulting in a more cohesive reporting of all the results.

Bivariate Correlations

This chapter begins by presenting bivariate correlations for the relevant variables. Analyzing bivariate correlations allows the researcher to assess the strength of relationships within a model without controlling for any other variables. Bivariate correlations alone are insufficient to show relationships between two variables or to conclude that one variable has an effect on another; however, they can reveal preliminary relationships and identify any multicollinearity that may be present between independent variables.

Table 19 displays the correlation matrix for the variables in the analysis. There were several independent variables that were correlated with each other. Strong relationships were found between officers in the U.K. and officer-related independent variables. Officers in the U.K. were younger, less educated, less experienced, and less likely to be armed. Interestingly, older officers in both countries were more productive than younger officers.

Additionally, a strong relationship was found between officer age and level of experience. It is reasonable to assume that age and experience would be strongly related since officers must be older to have more years of experience behind them. When variables are highly correlated in a multiple regression analysis, it becomes problematic to discern the individual contribution of each variable when predicting the dependent variable(s) because the highly correlated variables are predicting the same variance in the dependent variable. The information in Table 19 supports this notion with a correlation coefficient of .89 between these two variables.

Due to the possibility of multicollinearity, model diagnostics procedures were performed and the results indicated that collinearity between these two variables was not problematic.[46] The variance

---

[46] When two independent variables are highly correlated (above .90), the risk of multicollinearity becomes greater (Tabachnick and Fidell, 2007). Although the correlation coefficient was below this threshold, it was close enough to warrant performing multicollinearity diagnostics procedures.

inflation factors were all below 1 and tolerance estimates all exceeded .70. These procedures confirm that the observed correlations between these two independent variables should not influence the regression estimates due to collinearity.

Among the dependent variables in the analysis, experiencing disrespect was found to have a negative relationship and anticipation was found to have a positive relationship with (quantitative) definitional inclusivity. In other words, officers in both countries who experienced more disrespect in encounters included fewer behaviors in their quantitative definition of disrespect. Additionally, officers who had more behaviors in their definition of quantitative disrespect anticipated disrespect more often.

Several bivariate relationships were found between the specific independent and dependent variables. U.K. officers anticipated disrespect more but had a less inclusive definition of disrespect, contrary to what was hypothesized. Armed officers and productive officers were more likely to have a more inclusive definition of disrespect. As hypothesized, officers who were cynical were more likely to experience disrespect during encounters but officers with more time on the job were also more likely to experience disrespect during encounters, contrary to what was hypothesized.

Anticipation of Disrespect

It was hypothesized that police officers in the U.K. would anticipate disrespect less often than police officers in the U.S. (H10) and that unarmed U.K. officers would anticipate disrespect more often than armed U.K. officers (H2).[47] Separate logistic regression equations were estimated and the results are reported in Table 20. While the first model is cross-national and the second includes only U.K. officers, these two hypotheses were placed within the same table because they are the only hypotheses which address anticipation of disrespect. All other hypotheses focus on definitional inclusivity or the perception of experiencing disrespect.

The descriptive statistics also revealed that this specific dependent variable included 26 cases with missing data, a much higher rate of missing information than the other dependent variables in the analysis.

---

[47] U.S. police officers were excluded from this specific analysis.

Table 19. Correlation Matrix for Study Variables (N=171)

	1	2	3	4	5	6	7	8	9	10	11	12
1. Country	1.000	.111	-.307**	-.182*	-.248**	-.565**	-.054	.030	.075	.177*	-.109	-.323**
2. White male		1.000	-.248**	.166*	.135	-.041	.010	.069	.027	-.046	.088	-.073
3. Education			1.000	-.117	-.047	.147	-.050	.028	.122	.318**	-.205**	.118
4. Experience				1.000	.897**	.101	.085	.100	.210**	-.056	-.024	.010
5. Age					1.000	.184*	.208**	.064	.121	-.071	-.058	.057
6. Armed						1.000	.096	.122	.002	-.096	.016	.157*
7. Productivity							1.000	.039	.114	.100	-.295**	.069
8. Cynicism								1.000	.227**	.093	-.138	-.052
9. Disrespect - Experience									1.000	-.150	-.257**	-.063
10. Disrespect - Anticipation										1.000	.178*	-.061
11. Inclusivity - Quantitative											1.000	.131
12. Inclusivity - Qualitative												1.000

Due to its original distributional form (see Chapter IV for discussion), this dependent variable is measured dichotomously (1= anticipated disrespect in every encounter type, 0=anticipated disrespect in less than every encounter type). The results of the logistic regressions are presented below in Table 20.

The descriptive statistics for this dependent variable (antidich) also revealed that the distributions were skewed to the left, primarily due to the fact that 39.7% of all officers (see Figure 4 in Chapter IV) anticipated disrespect in all encounter types. After the logistic regression equations were estimated, a Poisson regression equation was estimated on each as a test of robustness.[48] The results of the Poisson regressions were in concordance with the results of the logistic regression.

It was hypothesized that officers in the U.K. would anticipate disrespect less often than officers in the U.S. When justifying this hypothesis, an assumption was made regarding the nature of interactions in the U.K. It was believed that U.K. officers would anticipate disrespect less due to the fact that that they would experience fewer encounters where the citizen was disrespectful. It is reasonable to assert that if they experience disrespect less often, they would have less reason to anticipate it because encounters are generally more civil. A logistic regression was performed, the results of which are shown in model 1 of Table 20. The estimates show a relationship between country and anticipation in the opposite direction but the relationship was weak; the odds ratio of anticipating disrespect was .881 signifying that anticipation is 11.9% less likely with U.S. officers than with U.K. officers. Given the weak relationship, this hypothesis was not supported.

---

[48] Poisson regression can accommodate for skewness but the distribution must be skewed to the right rather than the left. The dependent (antidich) was skewed to the right which allowed for a Poisson regression equations to be estimated and allowed for verification of the logistic regressions.

Table 20: Multivariate Models Estimating Anticipation of Disrespect. Model 1: U.S. Officers and U.K. Officers. Model 2: Armed U.K. Officers and Unarmed U.K. Officers

Dependent Variables	Model 1 Anticipation of Disrespect B (SE) [eβ]	Model 2 Anticipation of Disrespect B (SE) [eβ]
Intercept	-1.063	.928
Independent Variables		
U.K. Officers	-.126 (.381) [.881]	--- ---
Armed U.K. Officers	--- ---	-1.63 (.801) [.195]
Control Variables		
White	-.610 (.580) [.544]	.284 (1.04) [1.33]
Male	-.307 (.553) [.736]	1.688 (.977) [5.40]
Education	.327 (.157) [1.387]	-.075 (.284) [.928]
Experience	-.034 (.026) [966]	-.018 (.048) [.982]

a. Model 1: Logistic regression comparing U.S. officers and U.K. officers: N=142.
b. Model 2: Logistic regression comparing only armed UK. officers and unarmed U.K. officers: N=68.

In light of these results, the assertion that U.K. officers would anticipate less disrespect due to fewer experiences with disrespectful citizens might be inaccurate. In fact, higher levels of anticipation with U.K. officers may be the result of fewer experiences with disrespectful citizens. As noted in Chapter 5, the higher levels of anticipation in U.K.

officers could be driven by the lower violent crime rate in the U.K. and the smaller number of violent or dangerous calls that U.K. officers are sent to. The firearms specialists would be the only officers who respond to the dangerous crime calls and would anticipate disrespect due to the unpredictable nature of the calls. Vehicle and foot patrol officers would also anticipate disrespect more often since they have a reduced chance of encountering dangerous citizens/suspects or unpredictable encounters. In other words, fewer violent or dangerous calls could yield higher levels of uncertainty prior to encounters and subsequently, U.K. officers could anticipate disrespect more.

It is also possible that this result is due to the fact that the majority of officers in this sample are assigned to foot patrol. Foot patrol officers encounter more citizens on a daily basis and may be more likely to formally or informally sanction citizens for minor offenses. Officers may expect that citizens will feel as if these intrusions are trivial and given this, these officers may be more likely to anticipate disrespect in these low level encounters.

Moreover, foot patrol officers respond to requests when police community support officers (PCSO) have detained a citizen for minor offenses (see Crawford 2008).[49] The possibility exists that citizens may feel irate or annoyed that they are being detained by a PCSO and by the time a sworn officer arrives, those officers may be preparing themselves for the possibility that they will encounter a citizen who is more likely to exhibit verbally disrespectful behaviors toward them. Future analyses in this area should include PCSO's to explore their levels of anticipation and experience, and encounters in which PCSO's detain citizens while waiting for a sworn officer.

It is interesting to note that experience had a negative relationship with anticipation of disrespect. As years of experience increased, officers in both countries anticipated disrespect less often than those who have fewer years on the job; Anticipation is 65.5% less likely with experienced officers compared to those with less experience. This finding is noteworthy because it is not consistent with many of the

---

[49] PCSO's are non-sworn civilians whose aim is to reassure the public by providing a more visible police presence and to contend with low-level anti-social behavior. They also have the power to detain a citizen for 30 minutes pending the arrival of a sworn police officer (see Crawford, 2008).

equations assessing officers' perceptions of disrespect. Even though several of the later analyses found that experienced officers perceive disrespect more often, this result implies that those experiences may have little to do with whether or not they anticipate disrespect prior to entering into those encounters.

It was also hypothesized that armed officers in the U.K. would be less likely to anticipate disrespect compared to unarmed U.K. officers.[50] Since approximately 90% of officers in the U.K. are unarmed, it is reasonable to presume that the presence of a sidearm would inhibit disrespectful conduct from citizens. The results of the logistic regression (see Table 20, model 2) show a strong relationship in the predicted direction. The odds ratio was .195 which indicates that anticipation is .195 times less likely with armed U.K. officers. So the odds of anticipation decrease by 80.5% which signifies that unarmed U.K. officers anticipate disrespect more often than armed U.K. officers as hypothesized.

The descriptive results revealed that U.K. officers anticipated disrespect in all encounter types and had higher levels of anticipation than U.S. officers in most encounter types. U.K. officers enter into many encounter types expecting that they will encounter disrespectful citizens and the results of this analysis imply that a strong difference exists with how often armed and unarmed officers in the U.K. anticipate disrespect. Even though U.K. officers have high levels of anticipation overall, any practical considerations are made easier since the higher levels of anticipation come from unarmed officers who make up approximately 90% of all officers in the field. As such, any modifications to training or policies to reduce levels of anticipation can be made department-wide and those armed officers would benefit along with unarmed officers.

One other noteworthy finding must be addressed. The logistic regression revealed that male officers in London anticipated disrespect at a much higher rate than female officers. The odds of anticipation increased by 440.9% for male officers. While it is important to understand why male officers in London anticipate disrespect at much

---

[50] Since all officers in the U.S. sample carried a firearm, they were excluded from this analysis. Armed U.K. officers are only being compared to unarmed U.K. officers.

higher levels than female officers, it would be prudent to replicate this finding with a sample that included a higher percentage of female officers. Female officers comprised only 7% of the current London sample (compared to 22% in the entire MET).

Definitional Inclusivity

Aggregate Results

It is hypothesized that police officers in the U.K. will have a more inclusive definition of disrespect than police officers in the U.S. (H_{11}). In other words, officers in the U.K. will have a larger number of specific behaviors that they deem to be disrespectful compared to U.S. officers. For this hypothesis, two dependent variables were formed. The first was a qualitatively-based variable which was formed by the open-ended survey question which asked officers to list behaviors that they perceived as disrespectful prior to seeing any list of behaviors (DQsum). After officers responded to this question, they were given a list of behaviors and asked to identify the ones they deemed to be disrespectful. The quantitative measure of definitional inclusivity was formed based on the responses to this second question (DSsum).

Both dependent variables were formed in the same manner. Each of the behaviors were coded in a binary fashion (disrespectful =1, not disrespectful =0) and then summed to create a variety score. The higher scores signified more behaviors deemed to be disrespectful by each officer. This process yielded two distinct dependent variables, one based on officers' qualitative responses (DQsum) and the other based on officers' quantitative responses from the list provided to them (DSsum).

For this hypothesis, three distinct models were originally regressed to assess definitional inclusivity. The results are presented in Table 21. Two OLS regression equations were run, the first assessing the effect of officer's qualitative definition (model 1) and the second assessing officer's quantitative definition (model 2). The descriptive statistics also revealed two outlier values in officer's quantitative definition of disrespect which skewed the distribution to the left. As these outlier values could influence the regression coefficients, they were eliminated and a third model was regressed as a sensitivity test.

Table 21. Multivariate Models Estimating Definitional Inclusivity: Aggregate Disrespect

Dependent Variables	Model 1 Qualitative Definition β (SE)	Model 2 Quantitative Definition β (SE)	Model 3 Quantitative Definition* β (SE)
Constant	7.728 (1.43)	14.560 (1.834)	14.643 (1.596)
Independent Variable			
U.K Officers	-.304* (.431)	-.177 (.553)	-.164 (.478)
Control Variables			
White	.050 (.601)	.027 (.773)	-.022 (.674)
Male	-.116 (.625)	.038 (.803)	.105 (.689)
Education	.006 (.175)	-.260* (.225)	-.191 (.196)
Experience	-.043 (.028)	-.080 (.036)	-.156 (.031)

a. Model 1: R^2 = .113, Adjusted R^2 = .085. N=164.
b. Model 2 R^2 = .066, Adjusted R^2 = .036. N=164.
c. Model 3: *OLS regression of quantitative definition with elimination of outlier values. R^2 =.060, Adjusted R^2 =.029. N=162.
d. Effect size denoted as: *es>.20, **es>.50, ***es>.80.

It was hypothesized that officers in the U.K. would include more behaviors in their definition of disrespect. When controlling for other factors, this proposition was not supported (see Table 21). With the qualitative definition, U.S. officers had a more inclusive definitions but this relationship is weak. With both quantitative models, no relationship was found. When justifying this hypothesis, it was asserted that U.K. officers would include more behaviors in their definition because they may experience them less often. If a behavior occurs less often in police encounters, officers may be more likely to see that behavior as disrespectful since it is outside the norms of what officers deem to be acceptable. Instead, U.S. officer's more inclusive definition may be a product of the different types of behaviors that they encounter compared to U.K. officers. As noted in Chapter 5, U.S. officers had a wider variety of behaviors that they experienced on a regular basis and almost 20% of the behaviors they found to be most egregious were 'other' verbal behaviors such as talking on a cell phone or implying that the officer was dishonest.

Another explanation for this result may stem from the relationship between the anticipation of disrespect and the most common behaviors that officers encounter. U.K. officers anticipate disrespect in more encounter types (see Chapter 5, Table 9) but the behaviors they actually encounter more often may be more limited than in the U.S. For example, the most common form of disrespect exhibited by U.K. citizens in eight of ten encounter types was impoliteness. Compared to a wider variety of behaviors that U.S. officers experience more often, the fact that U.K. officers experience impoliteness so much may lead to a definition that includes fewer behaviors. Even with these results, it is important to note that the amount of variation explained by these equations was low. So even though the regression equations revealed a relationship between these two variables, an officer's country can only be considered a weak to modest predictor of definitional inclusivity.

The level of an officer's education influenced definitional inclusivity with their quantitative responses. In earlier analyses, it was found that as an officer's level of education increased, anticipating disrespect also increased slightly but when assessing definitional inclusivity, more educated officers actually included fewer behaviors in their quantitative definition of disrespect. When the outliers were removed (Table 21, model 3), the negative relationship remained but the effect size decreased to below .20.

The aggregate results presented above show that U.S. officers have a more inclusive definition of disrespect than U.K. officers in one model while the other two models revealed no relationships. While these results are clearly mixed, the aggregate results may not be specific enough in the effort to assess definitional inclusivity. Given that verbally disrespectful behaviors occur more often than physical ones, the possibility exists that differences in officers' verbal definitions may drive this relationship. As such, verbal indicators were separated from physical ones for analysis.

Verbal and Physical Disrespect

It was originally hypothesized that officers in the U.K. would have a more inclusive definition of disrespect. In the aggregate analysis, it was found that U.S. officers' definitions were more inclusive, contrary to what was hypothesized. The aggregate analysis alone however, may not tell the entire story. Verbally disrespectful behaviors are more common in both countries and U.K. officers reported that impoliteness (the lower end of the seriousness spectrum for verbally disrespectful behaviors) was the most common affront in the majority of encounter types. Given this, it would be reasonable to expect that U.S. officers would include more behaviors in their verbal definition of disrespect. While this result would be more in line with the aggregate results reported above, it would still be contrary to the original hypothesis. In either case, it is important to disaggregate disrespect into its constituent parts to determine if differences exist among verbal and physical behaviors.

As seen in Table 22, officers in the U.S. did include more behaviors in their qualitative definition of verbal disrespect and quantitative definition of physical disrespect but overall, these relationships are weak. Moreover, no relationships were found in the other two models. This result was unexpected given that the descriptive analysis revealed that U.K. officers included a smaller range of behaviors that they experience on a regular basis. In relation to verbally disrespectful behaviors, U.K. officers indicated that impoliteness is the most frequent disrespectful behavior they encounter. Based on these results and those in the previous chapter, it could be an indication that U.K. officers believe that they will encounter impolite citizens in a higher percentage of encounters. With impoliteness occurring most often and being on the lower end of the seriousness spectrum, this could simplify organizational efforts to reduce the probability of sanctions based on disrespectful behaviors in the U.K.

The results for the physically disrespectful behaviors were mixed, similar to those presented above. These models indicated that U.S. officers included more physical behaviors in their quantitative definition of disrespect. This was inconsistent with the original hypothesis. The results for both types of disrespect were inconsistent between the open and close-ended questions. The directions of the relationships were the same but relationships were found in only two of the four models. This lack of consistency between the quantitative and qualitative results also held true for the other relevant variables. Overall, it would be difficult to make firm conclusions based on these results.

Table 22. Multivariate Models Estimating Definitional Inclusivity: Quantitative and Qualitative by Verbal and Physical Disrespect

Dependent Variables	Model 1 Quantitative Definition: Verbal Disrespect β (SE)	Model 2 Qualitative Definition: Verbal Disrespect β (SE)	Model 3 Quantitative Definition: Physical Disrespect β (SE)	Model 4 Qualitative Definition: Physical Disrespect β (SE)
Constant	7.696 (.740)	4.540 (1.027)	8.172 (.936)	3.168 (.706)
Independent Variable				
U.K Officers	-.094 (.219)	-.299* (.310)	-.250* (.277)	-.101 (.213)
Control Variables				
White	-.131 (.316)	.104 (.433)	-063 (.399)	-.066 (.298)
Male	.306* (.316)	-.043 (.449)	-.029 (.400)	-.166 (.309)
Education	-.110 (.090)	-.057 (.126)	-.194 (.114)	.062 (.087)
Experience	-.232* (.014)	-.102 (.020)	-.120 (.018)	.029 (.014)

a. Model 1: R^2 = .154, Adjusted R^2 = .126. N=160.
b. Model 2: R^2 = .086, Adjusted R^2 = .058. N=164.
c. Model 3: R^2 = .070, Adjusted R^2 = .040. N=160.
d. Model 4: R^2 = .059, Adjusted R^2 = .030. N=164.
e. Effect size denoted as: *es>.20, **es>.50, ***es>.80.

Behavior-Specific Models

In both the aggregate and categorized models, the results were mixed. As noted above, it is possible that the results of these models could have been driven by individual behaviors. When both the verbal and physical behavior-specific models were separately regressed via linear probability models,[51] the inconsistency continued. In short, most of the models regressed did not reveal any significant differences between U.S. and U.K. officers and the individual behaviors. To save space here, all of the models were placed in Appendices III and IV.

When the verbal behaviors were individually regressed, U.S. officers were found more likely than officers in the U.K. to believe that ignoring commands (qualitative), verbal antagonism (quantitative), and making a racially derogatory remark (qualitative) are disrespectful. This finding substantiates the descriptives results where more U.S. officers had a wider variety of behaviors in their definition and could be due to the fact that citizens in the U.K. may be more likely to display impoliteness in encounters in police-citizen encounters. Given the results reported above, the lack of consistency between the qualitative and quantitative models, and the fact that only three of the fourteen models indicated that relationships existed, it would not be reasonable to assert that the aggregate or categorized definitions of disrespect were driven by any specific behavior or grouped verbally disrespectful behaviors.

It is interesting that the relationship between country and impoliteness was not significant when run separately. In the U.K., impoliteness was the most common behavior in eight of ten encounter types (see Chapter 5, Table 14) and 94.4% of U.K. officers believed impoliteness to be disrespectful (see Chapter 5, Table 17). With this information, it would be logical to assume that more U.K. officers would include impoliteness in their definition of disrespect but this did not bear out in the analysis.

---

[51] A linear probability model is used when the dependent variable is coded in a binary fashion. In this study, the survey instrument instructed respondents to deem the specific behaviors as either disrespectful (coded as 1) or not (coded as 0). So while the aggregate models utilized a summed variety score of the disrespectful behaviors, the individual behaviors were coded in a binary fashion, necessitating the use of a linear probability model.

In relation to physically disrespectful behaviors, the results were similar. Only three of the models indicated a relationship with perception of disrespect. The relationship between country and specific physical behaviors (resisting arrest [qualitative and quantitative], taking a defensive stance [quantitative], and pursuit [quantitative]) were present but weak and indicated that U.S. officers were more likely to include these behaviors in their definition. Similar to the results reported above, little variation was explained in the models and most revealed no relationship between the specific behaviors and the country the officers work in

In all, the behavior-specific models do little to help explain the aggregate and categorized results above. Of all the behavior-specific models run, only twelve revealed relationships with officer's perception of disrespect and only six of those twelve related to country. Even though they were in line with the aggregate results, the inconsistencies and the fact that the relationships were weak make it unreasonable to put forth any assertions as to the strength of their contribution to the those models.

Summary of Hypothesis Testing

In this chapter, bivariate correlations were discussed as well as the results for three of the associational hypotheses. The bivariate correlations revealed mixed support for several hypotheses and no significant relationships between others. The correlation matrix also revealed independent variables that were highly correlated but in the explanatory analyses, multicollinearity was not found to be a problem.

The hypotheses related to anticipation of disrespect and definitional inclusivity were analyzed in this chapter. It was hypothesized that officers in the U.K. would anticipate disrespect less often than officers in the U.S. but the analysis revealed that U.K. officers anticipated disrespect more often (although the relationship was weak). It was also hypothesized that armed officers in the U.K. were more likely to anticipate disrespect than unarmed officers. The results revealed a strong relationship in the direction opposite of what was expected. Unarmed U.K. officers anticipated disrespect at a rate much higher than armed U.K. officers.

As shown by the results reported above, definitional inclusivity is difficult to pin down. The aggregate analysis revealed that U.S. officers had a more inclusive definition of disrespect than U.K. officers, contrary to what was hypothesized. When separating verbal and physical behaviors into their own categories and when item-specific models were run, the results were inconsistent. Unfortunately, it would be problematic to make generalizations regarding definitional inclusivity due to conflicting results and the relatively low amounts of variation explained in the models presented above.

Chapter 7

Perceptions of and Experiences with Disrespectful Citizens

Introduction

With a better appreciation of how officers in these two countries define and anticipate citizen disrespect, the focus will now turn to the perception of disrespect. For practical purposes, it is important to understand if specific factors exist that influence how often officers experience disrespect. For example, if the results reveal that officers who are more educated experience less disrespect, it could imply that they comport themselves in a manner that deters disrespectful citizen behavior. Additionally, if cynical officers perceive more disrespect, it could be the result of citizens who sense that distrust and respond in kind. In both cases and with the other hypotheses analyzed in this chapter, departments could gain a clear understanding of the characteristics that officers bring to encounters and could modify admission standards, and academy/in-service training regimens accordingly.

This chapter will be separated into three sections. The first section will focus on the demographic and background characteristics of officers and how those characteristics might influence the perception of citizen disrespect. It is hypothesized that older, more educated, and more experienced officers in both countries will perceive that they encounter more disrespectful citizens compared to each of their younger, less educated, and less experienced counterparts, respectively. It is also hypothesized that white male officers in the U.S. will perceive more disrespect than white male officers in the U.K.

The remainder of the analyses will assess whether other factors help explain the perception of disrespect over and above the background factors. The second section will examine the perception of encountering disrespect more generally by comparing officers from each country to determine if officers from one country perceive disrespect more than the other. It was hypothesized that U.S. officers will perceive that they experience more disrespect than U.K. officers.

The third section will examine the effect of occupational-based characteristics on disrespect while controlling for background factors. These hypotheses assert that cynical and productive officers in both countries will perceive more disrespect and that productive officers in the U.S. will perceive more disrespect than productive officers in the U.K. Lastly, it was hypothesized that armed officers in the U.K. will perceive more disrespect than unarmed officers in the U.K. With all the hypotheses, multivariate ordinary least squares regression was utilized and the results will be reported.

As a final note, all of the hypotheses analyzed and presented in this chapter will utilize perception of disrespect as the dependent variable. In the survey instrument, officers were asked how often they actually experienced disrespect from citizens in specific types of encounters.[52] As discussed in Chapter 4, officers responses to this set of questions were measured ordinally based on a four-point Likert scale.[53] The scores for each individual encounters were averaged and transformed into single continuous variable with a possible range of values from 1-4. This dependent variable represents encounters in which officers experienced disrespectful behaviors with higher values equating to more perception/experience with disrespect.

---

[52] Encounters included: Domestic disputes, violent crime calls, non-serious crime calls, drug crime calls, drunk and disorderly calls, suspicious persons calls, calls for service, pursuits, traffic stops-DUI, traffic stops-non DUI.

[53] Responses: Always [4], sometimes [3], rarely [2], never [1]. The number in parentheses represent the SPSS coding scheme.

Perception of Experiencing Disrespect
Effect of Officer-Related Characteristics
Age, Experience, and Education
Not all officers go into different situations in the same fashion. When thinking about which factors influence the behaviors of citizens, many studies have focused on characteristics of officers (see for example Friedrich, 1980; Worden, 1995). Even though characteristics of officers have not been thoroughly examined in causal research, they are factors that have a possibility of influencing encounters and their outcomes. Moreover, it is possible that the effect of officers' characteristics will be consistent among officers from different countries. In this research, hypotheses were formed asserting that certain officer-related characteristics would influence how often they experience disrespect.

It is reasonable to assert that older, more experienced officers perceive disrespect in encounters less often than younger, less experienced officers. These older, more experienced officers understand the job more completely and have the benefit of experiential wisdom. Having experience gives them the ability to be more comfortable on the job, and over a period of time, these officers may feel as if they have experienced almost everything, including disrespectful citizens. Their age and experience give them the skills to defuse potentially volatile situations since they have been in similar situations before. On the other hand, younger and less experienced officers may be entering into new types of encounters, not knowing exactly what to expect. This may lead these younger officers to be more assertive and more sensitive to possible disrespectful behaviors and as such, they may be more likely to experience disrespectful citizens.

A similar assertion holds true for officers who are more educated. These officers may be more apt to use de-escalation skills in much of the same way as experienced officers. College educated officers may also be more tolerant to diverse viewpoints, ones that they may have experienced in the class or dormitory setting. Like experienced officers, their tolerance and communication skills give them a stronger ability to act in a conciliatory fashion when they believe encounters are moving toward conflict between them and the citizen or suspect.

As such, it was hypothesized that these characteristics would influence whether officers in both countries experience disrespect more often. The hypotheses are listed below:

H_6: In both countries, police officers who are older will experience disrespect less often than younger police officers.

H_7: In both countries, police officers who are more experienced will experience disrespect less often than less experienced police officers.

H_8: In both countries, more educated police officers will experience disrespect less often than less educated police officers.

OLS regressions were performed and the results are listed below (see Table 23).

Table 23: Multivariate Model Estimating the Effect of Officer-Related Characteristics on Disrespect

Dependent Variable	Citizen Disrespect (a) β (SE)
Constant	2.485 (.338)
Independent Variables	
Age	-.057 (.011)
Experience	.653** (.012)
Education	.271* (.028)
Control Variables	
White	-.070 (.103)
Male	-.080 (.105)

a. $R^2 = .118$, Adjusted $R^2 = .089$. N=157.
b. Effect size denoted as: *es>.20, **es>.50, ***es>.80.

First, officer age had no effect on citizen disrespect. In other words, age is not related to how often officers perceive disrespect from citizens. Additionally, education had a weak relationship and experience had moderate relationship to citizen disrespect. Officers with a higher level of education and more experience perceived more disrespect from citizens than officers with less education or experience. These results were contrary to what was hypothesized.

It was hypothesized that older, more experienced officers would perceive less disrespect. It is reasonable to assert that these officers are more comfortable and familiar with the variety of situations that they come across and hence less likely to allow situations move toward volatility (i.e. disrespectful behavior). The connection between disrespect, and age and experience was also expected given the strong positive bivariate relationship between age and experience (see Chapter 6, Table 19).

In regards to the level of experience an officer has, the results indicate that as the level of experience increases, the amount of disrespect that officers encounter also increases. Additionally and unlike more educated officers (see below), these experienced officers did not anticipate disrespect (see Chapter 6, Table 20) and they did not have a more inclusive definition of disrespect (see Chapter 6, Table 21) compared to less experienced officers. Based on this, experience as a predictor seems to stand alone rather than be mitigated by other factors such as anticipation or definitional inclusivity.

While contrary to what was hypothesized, the positive relationship between level of experience and perception of disrespect makes sense. Skolnick (1966) put forth that danger and authority were fundamental to the police occupation and environment, and as they progress in their time on the job, they become more suspicious, almost hyper-aware of those who may break the law (Skolnick's 'symbolic assailant'). Their experience actually separates them from citizens more than less experienced officers and may create an environment where officers perceive that verbal or physical resistance will occur. In these situations, more experienced officers may be more likely to see citizens as symbolic assailants and hence be more likely to perceive disrespect.

Interestingly, while experience did have a positive relationship with disrespect, age did not. Practically, this result is desirable since it signifies that younger officers may be receiving similar amounts of disrespect as older officers. This is especially important given that they may be more authoritative or assertive in encounters and hence more likely to induce disrespectful responses from citizens. Like productivity, this may indicate that citizens act or react equally to officers without regard to age.

The OLS regression also revealed that as officer's level of education increases, the amount of disrespect the officers perceive also increases, contrary to what was hypothesized. Educated officers may simply expect citizens to comport themselves in a more rational and reasonable manner and when citizens move outside the bounds of what those officers consider to be reasonable, it is deemed disrespectful. Given that they perceive disrespect more often, it would also be reasonable to assume that educated officers had a more inclusive definition of disrespect. Interestingly, the opposite is true. Educated officers actually had a (quantitative) definition of disrespect that included fewer behaviors.[54] This implies that they perceive more disrespect but with fewer behaviors that they deem to be disrespectful.

This relationship could stem from the climate within the educational system in the U.K. Like the educational environments in most countries, the school setting in the U.K. is one that is based within the larger set of cultural norms and it is likely that norms of communication and appropriate conduct are taught within the school. In a sense, students in the U.K. are taught in the classroom and via the school environment how they should comport themselves in the larger society. Those efforts at socialization carry over to modes of communication outside of school. In the university setting, these assertions would carry even more weight since the students are older and are now comporting themselves in a less structured environment.

The questions then become: How does the educational system in the U.K. differ from that in the U.S. and how might that affect officer's perceptions of disrespect of officers in the individual countries? There are general differences in the style of teaching and learning but the primary difference may stem from the impact of cultural norms of communication in schools and universities. While there is no empirical support for such an assertion, it would be illogical to believe that

---

[54] No relationship was found between an officer's education and their definition of disrespect.

conduct norms and expectations disappear when students enter into a school or university classroom (but see Beaudoin and Taylor, 2004).

Even with these results, it is important to note that the amount of variation explained by these equations was low. Moreover, even though the regression equations revealed relationships, the relationships were not strong. An officer's experience can only be considered a modestly strong predictor and education can only be considered a weak predictor of citizen disrespect.

White Males

Throughout the analysis, gender and race have both been used as control variables. When working to determine if the race and gender of officers influence the amount of disrespect they experience, the results of this research would be misleading if these two variables were utilized since both departments are primarily made up of white males. In the Oak Ridge and London samples, white male officers accounted for 75.6% and 84.4% of all officers, respectively.

As such, a dummy variable was created for this analysis distinguishing white males from all other sample participants. Given that it was hypothesized that white male police officers in the U.S. will experience disrespect more often than white male police officers in the U.K. (H_9), an interaction term was created to determine if there is an additive effect of both country and white males on citizen disrespect.

As Table 24 shows, this hypothesis was not supported. The white/male interaction term signifies that being a white male officer in the U.K. is less strongly correlated with disrespect (compared to U.S. officers) but the relationship as weak. Given that the weak relationship between white males and disrespect in the U.S., the interaction between country and white male was also weak. This indicates that there is no additive effect of white males and country on disrespect. Like several of the other unsupported hypotheses, this result is desirable, in a practical sense. In relation to the influence of officers' demographic characteristics on citizen behavior, race and gender are clearly the most noticeable physical characteristics to citizens, certainly compared to education or experience. If citizens are not being disrespectful to white male officers compared to other groups, it implies that citizens see officers as officers first, with little regard to the race and gender of officers. As such, if they choose to be disrespectful, their disrespect is aimed toward police officers more generally and not due to the race or gender of officers.

Table 24. Multivariate Model Estimating the Effect of a Country/White Male Interaction on Disrespect

Dependent Variable	Model 1 Citizen Disrespect β (SE)
Constant	1.614 (.148)
Independent Variables	
White Male	-.007 (.096)
U.K.	.030 (.208)
White Male/Country (U.K.) Interaction Term	-.050 (.212)
Control Variables	
Education	.230* (.031)
Experience	.157 (.005)

a. R^2 =.072, Adjusted R^2 =.041. N=157.
b. Effect size denoted as: *es>.20, **es>.50, ***es>.80.

Country Comparison

It was hypothesized that police officers in the U.S. would experience disrespectful behavior more often than police officers in the U.K. (H_{12}). As Table 25 indicates, the OLS regression revealed no substantive relationship in the expected direction. This finding is interesting given that U.S. officers included more behaviors in their definition of disrespect. It would be reasonable to assume that officers would experience more disrespect if they included more behaviors in their definition but this relationship did not bear out in the analysis.

Table 25: Multivariate Model Estimating the Effect of Country on Citizen Disrespect

Dependent Variable	Citizen Disrespect (a) β (SE)
Constant	1.894 (.249)
Independent Variables	
U.K. Officers	-.005 (.074)
Control Variables	
White	-.099 (.104)
Male	-.043 (.106)
Education	.223* (.030)
Experience	.178 (.005)

a. $R^2 = .082$, Adjusted $R^2 = .052$. N=157.
b. Effect size denoted as: *es>.20, **es>.50, ***es>.80.

When looking back at the descriptive results presented in chapter 5, the lack of a relationship makes more sense. The descriptive statistics revealed that experiencing disrespect was more prevalent in encounters where danger or unpredictability was a factor, or where the citizen was under the influence of alcohol. This was similar among officers from both countries and other than these two factors, the results were inconsistent. The descriptive analyses did not reveal that U.S. officers experienced more disrespect on a consistent basis. Disrespect seemed to vary more by encounter characteristics and citizen type rather than by country. Although the analysis did not reveal a relationship between country and disrespect, this result is not wholly unexpected given the mixed results presented in the Chapter 5.

While the hypothesis was not supported, education was found to be positively related to the perception of experiencing disrespect, consistent with the results presented above in Table 23. As level of education increased, so did experiences with disrespectful citizens. This finding is contrary to the results from both the definitional and anticipation-based hypothesis testing. In those analyses, increases in an officer's experience yielded fewer behaviors in their definition of disrespect and lower levels of anticipation (see Chapter 6, Tables 20 and 21).

Effect of Occupation-Related Characteristics
Armed/Unarmed Officers in the U.K
Close to 90% of officers in the U.K. and in the current sample do not carry firearms. Moreover, all armed officers are assigned to special vehicle patrol and none are assigned to foot patrol. As such, citizens are less likely to see an armed officer in the U.K. and the possibility of encountering an officer carrying a firearm might bring a stronger sense of submission on the citizen's part. Given this, it would be logical to hypothesize that armed U.K. officers would be less likely to experience disrespect than unarmed police officers in the U.K. (H_1). It must be reiterated that this hypothesis only compares armed and unarmed officers in the U.K.

Table 26: Multivariate Model Estimating the Effect of Armed U.K. Officers on Citizen Disrespect

Dependent Variable	Citizen Disrespect (a) β (SE)
Constant	1.476 (.335
Independent Variables	
Armed U.K. Officers	.093 (.041)
Control Variables	
White	-.048 (.143)
Male	-.035 (.126)
Education	.404* (.033)
Experience	.490* (.006)

a. R^2 =.327, Adjusted R^2 =.281. N=79.
c. Effect size denoted as: *es>.20, **es>.50, ***es>.80.

While the regression equation explained approximately 28% of the variation, the results of the OLS did not support this hypothesis (see Table 26). Instead, the effect coefficient revealed that armed officers experience slightly more disrespect but this relationship was weak. This could be due to the specialist nature of the armed U.K. officer's assignment. They respond primarily to potentially violent encounters where a citizen might be carrying a weapon and as such, might be likely to encounter suspects who are more willing to be disrespectful.

When thinking about the descriptives reported in Chapter 5, the results here seem reasonable. Armed U.K. officers are going to be the ones that respond to serious or violent crime calls. The descriptives revealed that 94.3% of U.K. officers anticipated disrespect in those types of calls (see Table 9a) and experienced disrespect in the majority of these calls (see Tables 10a, 11a, and 12a). So with higher levels of reported anticipation and experiences in these types of encounters, it is understandable that armed officers would perceive disrespect at slightly higher levels than unarmed officers.

Table 26 also reveals a small positive relationship between disrespect and an officer's education and experience. This has been the case with other equations in this research but these specific results are particularly noteworthy. First, 28.1% of the variation of disrespect was explained by this equation. Second, it strongly suggests that earlier equations where education and experience were found to be positively related were driven by U.K. officers. To confirm this, the effect of officer demographics (race, gender, education, and experience) on disrespect was regressed separately for officers in each country. The results confirmed that the relationship between education and experience, and disrespect is driven by officers in the U.K.[55]

Productivity and Cynicism

When thinking about how situations can influence decision making, an officer's attitude or approach to a citizen could influence the outcome of an encounter. In a sense, police officers present themselves to

---

[55] U.S. officers: education and experience were not related to disrespect and with these variables, only 2.4% of the variation in disrespect was explained. U.K. officers: education (β =.428) and experience (β =.721) were modestly related to disrespect and 29.7% of the variation in disrespect was explained.

citizens in social, albeit involuntary, situations. For example, productive officers may be more likely to approach citizens with an arrest or citation already in mind regardless of any other factors, including the citizen's behavior. Similarly, cynical officers may approach citizens with the mindset that the citizen will lie or attempt to deceive them. In either case, the tactics an officer might take could influence how often they experience disrespect. Any disrespect they encounter may be due to the officer's actions or attitude that give rise to the citizen's disrespectful behavior in the first place.

Table 27: Multivariate Models Estimating the Effect of Productivity and Cynicism on Citizen Disrespect

Dependent Variables	Model 1 Citizen Disrespect β (SE)	Model 2 Citizen Disrespect β (SE)
Constant	1.842 (.259)	1.951 (.249)
Independent Variables		
Productivity	.079 (.034)	--- ---
Cynicism	--- ---	-.005 (.026)
Control Variables		
White	-.102 (.102)	-.097 (.103)
Male	-.088 (.107)	-.081 (.109)
Education	.219* (.028)	.213* (.028)
Experience	.011 (.005)	.178 (.005)

a. Model 1: R^2 =.098, Adjusted R^2 =.068. N=154.
b. Model 2: R^2 =.083, Adjusted R^2 =.052. N=156.
c. Effect size denoted as: *es>.20, **es>.50, ***es>.80.

It was hypothesized that productive officers in both countries would be more likely to experience disrespect but this hypothesis was not supported (see Table 27). Even though the hypothesis was not supported, these results have important practical implications. These results suggest that officers who are more proactive and make more arrests compared to their peers are no more likely to perceive that citizens are acting disrespectfully. With involuntary encounters, the hope is that citizens and officers will not behave in such a way as to intensify the volatility of an already involuntary encounter. If productive officers do not perceive more disrespect, it suggests that they may not be overly assertive or aggressive in such a way as to warrant disrespectful behaviors or responses from citizens.

Another explanation for these findings could exist. While one could see where more arrest activity might yield more disrespectful citizens, the possibility exists that productive officers experience these behaviors but do not deem them to be disrespectful. Bivariate regressions testing the effect of productivity on definitional inclusivity were estimated to test this possibility. The results revealed that productive officers included fewer behaviors in their (quantitative) definition of disrespect.[56]

Based on these results, one can also assert that frustration and cynicism, central facets of police culture (see Skolnick and Fyfe, 1993) do not influence the perception of encountering citizen disrespect. Cynical officers were also hypothesized to experience more disrespect from citizens but like productivity, the OLS results revealed no relationship and this hypothesis was not supported. This suggests that officers in both countries may go into encounters with a cynical outlook but that they may not behaviorally express their cynicism. It may also suggest that citizens do not perceive an officer's cynicism or that they do not react to it if they do perceive it.

These results also suggest that an officer's behavior (productivity) or attitude (cynicism) may not temporally precede disrespect. Productive officers may experience disrespect simply because they arrest more suspects or are more proactive. Likewise, cynical officers may experience more disrespect because they may go into encounters

---

[56] β =-.324. The same analysis was completed on officer's qualitative definition of disrespect but no relationship was found.

frustrated or with a cynical outlook. They simply may be more sensitive to certain citizen behaviors. With this, the possibility exists that the officer's behavior facilitates or temporally precedes any disrespectful behavior or reaction from citizens or suspects. If productive and cynical officers do not perceive more disrespect, as this research has found, it implies that their behavior may not be offensive to citizens and hence does not warrant a disrespectful response. If a citizen's antagonistic demeanor or disrespect increases the probability of arrest and use of force, it is important to understand that the disrespect may not be a consequence of an officer's behavior or outlook.

In all, these are important findings because concern has been shown in relation to the effect that cynicism may have in encounters. While little research has been completed in the U.K., most of the research in the U.S. in this area focuses on the probabilities of arrest and use of force. When thinking about this specific research, the results reported here are important since they examine the citizen behavior (disrespect) that may come temporally before an arrest or use of force. These results suggest, then, that disrespect may not be an intervening variable between productivity or cynicism, and arrest or use of force.

There is also an important cross-national implication in that there was no appreciable difference between officers in each country. Initially, the productivity analysis presented was regressed without including country as a control variable. When country was added as a control, the results of the original analysis did not change. This may be inadequate to measure the influence of country since country and productivity could have an additive effect on citizen disrespect. Based on this, it was hypothesized that productive police officers in the U.S. would have a higher probability of experiencing disrespect than productive police officers in the U.K. (H_4).

As Table 28 shows, there is no relationship between productivity and disrespect among U.S. officers, contrary to what was hypothesized. The productivity/country interaction term describes how much (more or less) strongly productivity is correlated with citizen disrespect among U.K. officers (compared to U.S. officers), here .185 points higher. By adding these two coefficients together (productivity and productivity/country interaction term), it allows for recovery of the

overall relationship between productivity and disrespect in the U.K.,
here .197.

**Table 28. Multivariate Model Estimating the Effect of a
Country/Productivity Interaction on Disrespect**

Dependent Variable	Citizen Disrespect (a) β (SE)
Constant	1.90 (.285)
Independent Variables	
U.K.	-.190 (.233)
Productivity	.012 (.051)
Productivity/Country (U.K.) Interaction Term	.185 (.068)
Control Variables	
White	-.096 (.103)
Male	-.085 (.108)
Education	.225* (.030)
Experience	.204* (.005)

a. R^2 =.102, Adjusted R^2 =.059. N=154.
b. Effect size denoted as: *es>.20, **es>.50, ***es>.80.

In sum, the three hypotheses related to productivity and cynicism
were not supported but as noted above, the lack of support leads to
positive practical applications. Cynical and productive officers in both
countries do not experience more disrespect. Moreover, the results
indicated no significant differences between officers in the U.K. and
the U.S., implying that they are not entering into encounters with an
outlook or behavior that is noticeably different than their less
productive and cynical counterparts. As such, their behaviors are not
bringing about disrespectful responses from citizens.

Summary of Hypothesis Testing

In this chapter, the majority of the hypotheses were tested. All of these hypotheses examined the influence of certain characteristics on the perception of citizen disrespect; the influence of country, occupation-related characteristics, and officer-related characteristics. Based on the analyses presented above, none of these nine hypotheses were supported. Most revealed a relationship in the expected direction but were not strong (country, armed U.K. officers, productivity [both across countries and when comparing countries], and age). Two hypotheses revealed moderate relationships they were but not in the expected direction (education and experience), and two hypotheses resulted in weak relationships in the opposite direction (cynicism, white males).

As noted above, the value of this research is not diminished even though none of the hypotheses were supported. It was expected that citizen disrespect would vary according to different factors and while this was the goal of this specific research endeavor, there should be more interest and attention paid to the practical implications of these results. As this research has shown, only an officer's education and experience relate to how much disrespect they perceive, although the relationships were only moderately strong. No other factors influence how often officers perceive disrespect suggesting that both within and between countries, officers perceive that they encounter disrespect at similar rates. Given this, attention in departments must be paid to how officers more generally can work to reduce the incidences of disrespect that they come across. The following chapter will address this and other practical considerations.

Chapter 8.

Implications of the Findings

Introduction

There were two primary objectives of this research. First, the research sought to learn more about which behaviors officers in two countries deem to be disrespectful. The second objective was to cross-nationally compare officers' experiences with disrespectful citizens. This research is important because in the U.S., there is a body of research examining the influence of disrespect on officer decision making but flaws exist in how researchers conceptualize disrespect. In short, there is no research that has asked officers directly which behaviors they find to be disrespectful. In the U.K., there have been no studies assessing the influence of citizen disrespect on police decision making. This study sought to improve upon past research and to bridge these gaps in the literature.

Twelve distinct hypotheses were derived assessing the influence of specific factors on officer's definition of disrespect, their levels of anticipation, and how often they perceive disrespect from citizens. Learning more about the similarities and differences across countries and how they influenced officers' perceptions was of primary importance. As such, the twelve hypotheses centered on country-based factors, occupation-based factors, and officer-based factors.

With these factors in mind, this study makes valuable practical and methodological contributions. At the very least, it is essential to have a better understanding of the situations in which officers experience disrespect. Officers can use that information and enter into encounters with an idea of what disrespectful behaviors may occur. Additionally, this research helps gain a stronger understanding of the similarities and differences between officers in two distinct countries. With this information, officers in both countries can be trained to de-escalate situations where they experience disrespectful behaviors rather than sanction citizens with an arrest or use of force. Methodologically, researchers can utilize a conceptualization of disrespect based on behaviors that officers themselves deem to be disrespectful and this study can serve as a starting point for research assessing the effect on citizen disrespect in the U.K. Researchers can also use this information when comparing the police and police behavior in different countries and when assessing the effect of culture on police. These contributions/implications will be discussed after a brief review of the findings.

Review of the Findings

This study sought to gain a better understanding of officers' beliefs and perceptions of citizen disrespect and the extent to which disrespect occurs generally and in specific encounter types. Both descriptive and associational analyses were performed toward this purpose. The descriptive analyses focused primarily on the prevalence of disrespect in encounters, how often officers anticipate disrespect, and the most common and most egregious disrespectful behaviors officers encounter. Comparisons were made between U.S. and U.K. officers in these areas. The associational analyses sought to understand and cross-nationally compare the factors that influence officers' definitions of disrespect and their perceptions of disrespect in encounters. The descriptive analyses will be reviewed first followed by a review of the associational findings.

Review of the Descriptive Analyses

When examining the results of the descriptive analyses, clear and logical patterns emerged indicating that officers in both countries experienced citizens who exhibited disrespectful behaviors. First, officers indicated that verbally disrespectful behaviors were much more prevalent than physically disrespectful behaviors. Given the probability that physically disrespectful behaviors would be met with a physical response by the officer and the low percentage of encounters where physical force is used, this result was both logical and expected. Furthermore, most of the reported behaviors occurred at the low end of the seriousness spectrum (i.e. impoliteness) and officers in both countries agreed that the most egregious behaviors were spitting and physically assaulting an officer. The results were similar among officers in both countries.

When anticipation and perception of disrespect were broken down by encounter type, a clear trend emerged. Officers in both countries were more likely to perceive disrespect from citizens in encounters that were dangerous or ones where the citizen was intoxicated. With officers in the U.S., this pattern was clear but the trend was less obvious with officers in the U.K. In both countries, more officers experienced disrespect 'often' in domestic disputes, serious crime calls, drug offenses, drunk and disorderly calls, pursuits, and DUI's. Officers in both countries also indicated that they perceived disrespect at almost every drunk and disorderly call, drug offense call, and domestic dispute.

Similar to their perceptions of disrespect, patterns emerged when examining the encounters in which officers anticipated that they would experience disrespect prior to entering the encounter itself. The dangerous and unpredictable encounters were the ones where more officers anticipated a disrespectful citizen and it was interesting to find that U.K. officers had much higher rates of anticipation in these types of encounters. In fact, U.K. officers anticipated disrespect more than U.S. officers in the majority of encounter types, contrary to what was hypothesized.

When comparing definitional inclusivity among officers, the results suggest that officers in both countries have consistent views as to the types of behaviors they include. Both U.S. and U.K. officers included all the behaviors that have been utilized in past conceptualizations and many included 'talking on a cell phone' and 'making a racially derogatory statement.' This implies that past conceptualizations may not have been inclusive in relation to the behaviors they included in their definitions of disrespect. Officers in both countries also included behaviors that are not necessarily hostile (talking on a cell phone, ignoring commands or requests), ones that occur prior to any face-to-face interaction (pursuit, fleeing on foot), and illegal behaviors (assault, spits, and pursuit). These behaviors distinguish these results from past research and should be taken into consideration with future causal research in either country.

When thinking about the descriptive results, some clear patterns emerged and other results were mixed. One thing is certain; officers in both countries anticipate and perceive disrespect in encounters. Moreover, those perceptions are heightened when danger or sobriety is at issue. Officers in both countries also included the same behaviors in their definition of disrespect. While the results of the descriptive analyses were informative, the explanatory analyses also sought to shed more light on the factors that influenced officers' definitions, anticipation, and perceptions. These will be discussed in the next section.

Review of the Explanatory Analyses

Several hypotheses were put forward asserting that explanatory relationships would be found between disrespect and country-based factors, occupation-based factors, and officer-based factors. After performing all of the explanatory analyses, only one of the twelve hypotheses presented was supported. Since the explanatory analyses did reveal important, albeit unexpected relationships, the lack of support does not mitigate the contribution that this research makes.

Two hypotheses related to anticipation of disrespect were tested. It was first asserted that officers in the U.S. would anticipate disrespect more than officers in the U.K. A weak relationship was found opposite of what was predicted. When comparing levels of anticipation between armed and unarmed U.K. officers, it was found that unarmed officers anticipated disrespect more than armed officers. This was the only hypothesis in the research that was supported.

Definitional inclusivity was then examined with the assertion that U.K. officers would include more behaviors in their definition of disrespect. The analysis revealed that U.S. officers had a more inclusive definition of disrespect. When the aggregate definition was re-analyzed separating verbal and physical disrespect, each of the four tested models[57] did result in coefficients that were in the same direction as the aggregate model but only two of the four revealed moderately strong relationships.[58] When the behavior-specific models were

---

[57] Quantitative verbal, quantitative physical, qualitative verbal, qualitative physical.

[58] Qualitative verbal and quantitative physical.

examined, the results were also inconsistent. Moreover, most of the behavior-specific models found no relationships and the amount of variation explained was consistently low.

The remainder of the hypotheses tested officers' perceptions of disrespect and examined various factors that lead to how often they perceive disrespect. First, analyses were performed comparing officers' general perceptions of disrespect in the two countries and a second analysis compared only armed and unarmed U.K. officers. While both revealed relationships in the expected direction, neither were strong.

Further analyses were conducted on the hypotheses which asserted that occupational and officer-related characteristics would influence the perception of disrespect. It was hypothesized that productive and cynical officers in both countries would perceive more disrespect and that productive officers in the U.S would perceive more disrespect than productive officers in the U.K. None of these three were supported.

Officer-based characteristics were examined next. It was hypothesized that younger, less educated, and less experienced officers in both countries would perceive that they experience disrespect more often. Similar to the original country comparison, it was also asserted that white male officers in the U.S. would perceive more disrespect than white male officers in the U.K. In relation to age and the race-gender analyses, the results revealed relationships in the expected direction but neither were strong.

The analyses on the education and experience hypotheses, on the other hand, revealed interesting results. Both analyses revealed moderate relationships but ones that were opposite of what was expected in several of the models tested. In other words, both education and experience were positively related to the perception of disrespect. This will be addressed in more detail below.

Overall, there was little support for the hypotheses presented in this research. As noted above, however, the lack of significance does not detract from the contribution that this research makes to the extant literature. These contributions will be explained in more detail in the implications section below.

Implications

This study goes beyond extant research and makes a contribution in several respects. The practical implications for this study will be considered first followed by a discussion of utilizing officer surveys in studies that rely on a determination or classification of citizen behaviors by officers. The cross-national implications will be addressed last in this section.

Practical Implications

In encounters with citizens, officers in both countries are faced with discretionary choices at every stage, from contact to exit. With new information regarding what types of disrespectful behaviors are more prevalent generally and in different types of encounters, officers can be made more aware of the disrespectful behaviors they may encounter in different situations. Alone, this would be inadequate but if officers can be more aware of the behaviors they may encounter, they can work to avoid labeling the behaviors as personal affronts. Without the label, they are better equipped to avoid sanctioning a citizen based on the disrespectful behavior rather than the original offense or reason for the call. The question then becomes, how can the results of this research translate into practical, policy-related changes in police departments in the U.S. and in the U.K.?

Police Perceptions, Awareness and Discretionary Choices

In the end, an important goal of police research is to have an increased understanding of what influences police behavior. Prior to these determinations and changes in practice, however, a chronological step backward must be taken and police perceptions of disrespect must be examined in relation to policy changes. In other words, it is imperative to understand why and how officers react to certain citizen behaviors, in this case, disrespect. With a stronger basis of knowledge of how disrespect influences police decisions, police organizations can work to modify officers' behaviors and reactions when they face disrespect. Put differently, citizen disrespect is a factor that can influence the outcomes of police-citizen encounters and as such, it is important to understand how disrespect influences police decision making.

Organizationally, the implications are clear. At the very least, police administrators seek to maintain a positive relationship with the citizens they police as well as the media outlets that report on police behavior. A decrease in formal or informal sanctioning can lead to a decrease in citizen complaints and less negative attention, in whatever form. Fewer citizen complaints, regardless of whether they are deemed to be unfounded, help police chiefs in this effort. Moreover, front line supervisors will receive and investigate fewer complaints against officers in their command, and officers could find themselves in fewer volatile situations.

This implication is interesting when considering the behavioral norm differences in the two countries and how those differences might influence complaints from citizens. In the U.K., past research has shown that citizens are less likely to express dissatisfaction with a police officer until after the encounter is over (Maguire and Corbett, 1991; Walters and Brown, 2000) and that the police are expected to uphold the social and behavioral norms (Jackson and Bradford, 2009). Citizens may act disrespectfully (even unknowingly) and when reprimanded by the officer, the norms of acceptable behavior may lead them to modify their behavior to meet the officer's expectation of subservience. Moreover, officers in the U.K. may be more likely to respond with verbal commands, thereby giving the citizen the opportunity to reconsider their behavior. Since being non-confrontational is rooted in the U.K.'s norms of communication, these citizens might wait until later to complain to the officer's superior for fear of further confrontation. On the other hand, citizens in the U.S. may continue to act disrespectfully after a reprimand or may be more likely to complain during the encounter and this could increase the probability of future informal or formal sanctions. A cross-national study comparing officers' responses to disrespect could discover any differences between these two countries.

Thinking more about officers in the field, focus should be on the disrespectful behaviors that have been found to be more prevalent in specific encounter types. In every police-citizen encounter, from the initial contact to exit, there are discretionary choices that officers are faced with. Each individual choice an officer makes could have a marked effect on the way the encounter progresses. With this information, officers can be more aware of the likelihood of such behaviors and can act in such a way to prevent them from occurring. If citizens do act disrespectfully, officers can be prepared and can work to de-escalate encounters rather than resort to sanction.

This information may also be beneficial even if the behaviors are not ones that are in the officer-driven definition. While the research revealed a consistent definition of disrespect from officers in both countries, it is important to consider that all officers may not have a list of behaviors that exactly matches that of their fellow officers. So while this research formulated an officer-driven definition of disrespect that officers in both countries were in agreement with, it is likely that specific officers will have certain behaviors that they find disrespectful that others do not and those individual officers will be more aware of those behaviors when they occur (see Dunham and Alpert, 2009).

Knowing which behaviors occur more often during encounters is important but individual officers may also deem specific behaviors as disrespectful that do not occur on a regular basis (i.e. dropping another officer's name or implying that the officer is dishonest). Even though those specific behaviors may not be among the behaviors included in an officer-driven definition of disrespect, training can make officers more attentive to disrespectful behaviors more generally. Simply put, the training could make officers more aware of the types of disrespectful behaviors that they may experience during encounters and could give them options for responding to those behaviors or any different behaviors that they personally believe to be disrespectful.

Implications for Training

In both the U.S. and U.K., new officers must go through an extensive training regimen which includes both classroom and field training elements. In the academy setting, recruits would benefit if possible disrespectful behaviors and prevalence of those behaviors were addressed. While some officers are hired with previous police experience, few recruits in a rookie school have ever been a police officer and most current or retired officers would assert that those who have not been in the field cannot imagine what the job entails. A class or segment of a class on what officers in the field deem to be disrespectful and which encounter types they may be more likely to experience would be an appropriate starting point. This would give recruits the knowledge and ability to react positively to respectful behavior and avoid responding negatively to disrespectful behavior (see also Dunham and Alpert, 2009). Moreover, this could be strengthened and confirmed with role playing and street survival training in the academy setting, which are elements of training that are as close to real-life situations/encounters as most recruits in an academy will experience. This information might already be transmitted informally from training officers during these training segments but this might serve the unintended purpose of instructing cadets to sanction disrespectful offenders rather than teach them how to act or react appropriately when those behaviors occur.

Academy training should only be the starting point because many field training officers (FTO's) will instruct rookie officers to forget what they learned in the academy since it is not the same as being on the job. This formalized on-the-job training could serve as the most important time to train rookies in this area, particularly via a recruit's observations of the FTO's own actions and reactions when they experience disrespectful citizens.[59] With the growing emphasis on community oriented policing in both countries and the fact that both departments have a field training component, field training would certainly be an appropriate place to continue this type of training.

In both the academy setting and field training, new officers could be made aware of their own biases and personal dislikes. They may have certain behaviors that they perceive to be affronts and may respond negatively to those behaviors more than others (i.e. denying commands, using profanity). If they can be more aware of their own personal dislikes, then they will be better equipped when that behavior arises and can work toward de-escalation rather than toward an inappropriate sanction. Officers who are equipped to verbally de-escalate or negotiate will be in a much safer position than those who are not and if a reduction in violent police-citizen encounters is a continuing goal for police and researchers, then understanding the triggers and having the ability to verbally negotiate can work toward this goal.

Level of Education and Disrespect

In this analysis, the most unexpected result was that level of education was a predictor of citizen disrespect, contrary to what was hypothesized. The results indicated that officers in both countries who had a higher level of education perceived disrespect more often in

---

[59] FTO's should be trained in this area prior to being given a recruit.

encounters. Even though this relationship was driven by U.K. officers in this sample, it is still important to consider the possibility that educated officers have higher standards of communication that they hold citizens to. This result is also consistent with the finding that educated officers anticipated disrespect more often while at the same time, including fewer behaviors in their definition of disrespect. Future research in this area is warranted.

These results are important to consider given the increasing percentage of departments in the U.S. requiring at least some college (Pastore and Maguire, 2006).[60] Moreover, recruitment and promotion strategies in the U.K. have also seen an increased emphasis on educational qualifications in an effort to increase police professionalism (Newburn, 2008). At the current time, the MET does not require any college as a minimum eligibility requirement for becoming a police officer (Metropolitan Police, 2009) but this finding is important to consider given that 67.4% of the current sample had at least some college/university.

If educated officers in both countries are including fewer behaviors in their definition but are anticipating and perceiving disrespect more often, then particular attention must be given to these officers in training and in-service training. While this may be the result of educated officers having higher behavioral standards of communication and interaction than the citizens they encounter, they must not be ignored during training. In fact, it may be prudent for training programs to highlight the fact that these officers may perceive disrespect more often, making them more aware of their own behavioral biases.

Implications for Community Policing

To frame this discussion, reference must be made to the trends occurring in both departments. In both countries, the most prominent trend in policing is the move toward community oriented policing. The MET explicitly works to 'bridge the gap between citizens and the police' with the intention of working together with citizens 'for a safer

---

[60] In 2000, 15% of local police departments in the U.S. required at least 'some college' as a minimum educational requirement. In 2003, that percentage increased to 18% (Pastore and Maguire, 2006).

London.' They implement community policing via neighborhood watch, police community consultive groups, use of PCSO's, and safer neighborhood teams (Metropolitan Police, 2011). They actively campaign to decrease low level anti-social behavior and increase civility among the citizenry (see NPIA, 2010; Metropolitan Police 2011; Moore, 2011). By focusing on civil communication and a cooperative effort, the MET openly strives to facilitate and promote the relationship between citizens and the police. With the exception of the use of PCSO's, similar programs with similar goals are implemented in the U.S. and in Oak Ridge. While keeping citizens safe by preventing and responding to crime, reformers in both countries attempt to connect citizens and police with the goal of increasing community and citizen satisfaction with the police and police services.

When thinking about the rationales set forth for the hypotheses, an assertion could have been made suggesting that U.K. police officers and organizations would be more likely to engage in community policing. If the behavior of officers is expected to comport with values and customs of the country, it makes sense that U.K. officers would strive to communicate with citizens in a suitable and non-confrontational manner and that department policies would support this. Historically, this also makes sense since the roots of policing in the U.S. are primarily law enforcement related while the early police in the U.K. sought to reduce social disorder.

Practically, there are two discernable differences between these two departments. While Oak Ridge does have a strong community policing strategy, the MET has put a much higher percentage of their officers on foot patrol and they are more active in explicitly promoting and publicizing their efforts of bridging the gap between citizens and the police, increasing public confidence in police, and reducing a general level of anti-social behavior by its citizens (see Jackson and Bradford, 2009; Bradford, 2011; Moore, 2011). Through their policies and goals, the British government and the MET consciously and overtly promote civility in encounters in an attempt to emulate the appropriate normative level of communication in England (see Crawford 2009).

Even with these differences, the results of this study could influence the way in which departments in both countries strategically engage in community policing. Police departments and officers reach out to citizens in a variety of ways. From ride-alongs, citizen police academies, community resource officers in schools, and community meetings, citizens are afforded opportunities to interact with officers on a voluntary basis. These types of interactions are becoming much more common and in them, citizens can be made aware of what officers deem to be disrespectful with the ultimate goal of reducing the prevalence of such behaviors. Using a voluntary setting rather than a law enforcement-based situation to inform citizens is clearly more advantageous. Citizens would be more open to the information and could be made to understand how officers see and how they may react to disrespectful, without fear of sanction. Moreover, one could expect that declining rates public confidence could turn around and begin to increase.

While blame cannot be placed on citizens for inappropriate reactions to disrespect from officers, it would be beneficial to inform citizens as to what behaviors they should avoid when interacting with officers, especially when paying attention to how outcomes of situations can be influenced by certain citizen behaviors. For example, even though most citizens are aware that spitting on or assaulting an officer are illegal, they might not know that less insulting behaviors such as using profanity or talking on a cell phone can also be considered affronts to officers. The relationship between police and citizens could clearly benefit when citizens can be given information in voluntary interactions with police.

Cross-National Implications

The above discussions necessarily raise implications in relation to policing cross-nationally. Are police officers from these two countries similar and does the presence and characteristics of police subculture transcend borders? While not incontestable, the results of this research tend to support this notion. Officers in both countries had the same definition of disrespect, similar experiences with disrespect, and find similar behaviors to be more egregious than others. Additionally, the explanatory analyses revealed few differences among officers in the two countries and the differences that were found were officer-based rather than departmental or police subculture-based. So while an officer's education and experience influenced the perception of disrespect, it did so with officers from both countries and as such, this research supports the belief that police in these countries are similar on this dimension.

When thinking about the results cross-nationally, there are also important organizational implications even though all of the cross-national hypotheses were unsupported. For example, the results revealed no differences across countries in regards to productivity and no differences between officers in both countries who were productive or cynical. If cynical officers in both countries are experiencing similar amounts of disrespect, it could be asserted that these officers may not act differently than officers who are not cynical. In other words, an officer's cynical outlook may not translate into behavioral expressions of their cynicism toward citizens. If their behavior in encounters does not reflect their cynical outlook, then any disrespect from citizens that occurs may not be due to characteristics related to police subculture. Moreover, this lends credence to the assertion that police subculture and behavior is similar across national boundaries, specifically in relation to how cynicism influences behavior.

Since disrespect has been found to be a predictor of police use of physical force (in the U.S.), then this finding may call into question how cynicism relates to an officer's response to disrespectful behavior. If cynical officers go into encounters expecting the worst from citizens as Waddington (1993) suggests, then they may be more aware of potentially disrespectful behaviors. If they are more sensitive to specific citizen behaviors and tend to have a lower threshold of what they deem to be disrespectful, then one can assert that they would be more likely to sanction citizens for such behaviors. While this study did not examine officers' responses to disrespectful behavior, the results indicate that they are not experiencing more disrespect and suggests that if cynicism predicts use of force (Worden, 1995), then it may not be in response to a disrespectful citizen.

Additionally, productive officers in both countries were no more likely to perceive disrespect. When making the connection between disrespect as a predictor of use of force, this finding supports Toch's notion that violence prone officers are not necessarily productive ones (Toch, 1995). Instead, a higher likelihood to use force may be related more to characteristics other than productivity. Given this information, future research on police subculture could utilize the results of this study and could engage in a closer examination of the relationship between cynicism and productivity, citizen behavior, and officers' responses to that behavior.

As noted earlier, cross-national and comparative research has had relatively little impact on policy making, especially in relation to policing in the U.S. In the U.K., there has been almost no research in this area. So, even though little appreciable difference was found between these two organizations, comparatively examining the impact of occupation and officer-based variables has important implications for implementation and for study. Studies such as this one bring the focus back to officers' responses to disrespect instead of primarily focusing on the citizen's actions that lead to those responses. By doing so, it allows for policy change to begin from within departments rather than relying on citizens to change. In short, if it is inevitable that citizens will act disrespectfully, then the burden to modify behaviors and responses should lie with the officer and the department, rather than the citizens. Since both departments have a law enforcement focus with an increasing emphasis on community policing, it is important for officers in both organizations to be more aware of citizens' behaviors and their responses to them.

When looking at the bigger picture, the results also suggest that each country's norms, customs, and values did not play as strong a role as was hypothesized. It was believed that officers in the U.K. would have higher behavioral expectations of citizens and that those citizens would be less likely to move beyond the boundaries of acceptable behavior in encounters. This did not bear out in the analysis. Even with a strong focus on reducing anti-social behavior, few appreciable differences were found in the cross-national analyses and the same held true when comparing traits and characteristics across countries. In fact, the similarities revealed in the results tended to support the assertion that the norms and customs of each country may play a less important role in how officers define disrespect and how often they perceive it in encounters.

In both countries, the normative expectations that officers have in any given situation with citizens seem to stem more from the occupational roles and subculture of the police. So when thinking about how the different factors can affect outcomes, the results here would suggest that the characteristics of encounters in both countries may influence outcomes at similar rates. Put differently, the results suggest that future cross-national studies assessing the effect of disrespect on police decision making might not find significant differences between officers in these two countries.

Methodological Implications

When reviewing the research that has examined the effect of disrespect on police decision making, none have utilized officer surveys to understand what behaviors officers believe to be disrespectful. Relying on researcher-driven conceptualizations may adequately reflect the breadth of behaviors that make up disrespect in officer's eyes but as this research has shown, three issues are raised. First, each study in this area has utilized a different conceptualization of disrespect. Second, a body of research that utilizes differing conceptualizations may not, in effect, be measuring the same phenomenon. Third, previous conceptualizations have not included all of the behaviors that officers here found to be disrespectful. With differing conceptualizations and measurements of disrespect that are used for study, any broad conclusions made based on that research would be have to be deemed suspect.

In order to obtain reliable information that can be used in police research and toward policy change, research must be conducted using consistent conceptualizations that come from officers themselves. The limitations of surveys notwithstanding, understanding officers' views would be a dependable route to valid conceptualizations. Moreover, utilizing a valid conceptualization on a consistent basis would allow for a coherent body of research and a better understanding of the phenomenon being studied.

To understand how disrespect influences an officer's decision, one must understand what officers find to be disrespectful and this research worked toward that end. The use of officer-based conceptualizations need not end here, however. Use of physical force and excessive force conceptualizations could be improved upon as well as the different factors that can influence officer decisions, such as pretext stops by officers. In all, the use of officer surveys can be employed to establish consistent and valid measures of social phenomena in police research.

Chapter 9.
Present and Future Considerations

Introduction

This study has produced new information increasing understanding in police research by examining the behavioral indicators that officers give to disrespect resulting in an officer-driven conceptualization of disrespect. Additionally, more is now known regarding the factors that influence where and how often officers perceive disrespectful behaviors from citizens. The contributions to the comparative literature are equally important, especially in relation to how alike police are in different countries and the introduction of a new body of research which focuses on disrespect toward the police in the U.K.

This study is not without limitations and more research needs to be undertaken but this work and the results are valuable in that disrespect toward the police is a phenomenon that effects all police officers at some point in their career (or during each shift) and all police organizations. Since citizen disrespect has been found to influence police decision making and police use of force in specific, it is imperative that a thorough understanding of the occurrences and perceptions of disrespect be obtained. Given the trends of improving community relations in both countries, it is especially important that officers use legal factors to base their decisions on rather than extra-legal factors.

Limitations

This study revealed valuable information that adds to the literature and has practical applications. The contributions notwithstanding, it must be acknowledged that there are shortcomings to this research. With most studies, with recognition of limitations comes the caveat that the results must be viewed with caution. Here, that caveat centers around the ability to generalize these results to those agencies in the sample and to all police in the U.S. and U.K. This section will address the methodological and practical limitations of this research.

Methodologically, the sampling technique and the sample size are the two primary limitations. In this research, only two police departments were sampled and the resulting sample from these departments is relatively small (171 total officers in the sample; 79 in Oak Ridge and 92 in London). Given the number of officers in the sample (and the relatively low response rate), generalizability becomes an issue. It would be problematic to assert that all officers in all departments in both countries would have responded in a similar fashion to the survey instrument.

Moreover, individual officers who participated in the study were chosen through purposive sampling, a non-probabilistic sampling technique. Practical considerations did not allow for random sampling and as such, the results of the analyses may not reflect the views of the population of officers in each department. Caution must be taken when examining any significant results and the practical implications surrounding those results.

Lastly, veracity of responses may also be a concern. Police officers are historically cautious when revealing information about their views and behaviors and this can be especially problematic in survey research (see Maxfield and Babbie, 2011). Despite officer's reluctance, this drawback may be less of a concern due to the fact that officers were not asked how they responded to disrespectful behaviors when they encountered them. By not asking officers if they have acted improperly in the face of citizen disrespect, it allowed them to focus on their perceptions rather than worry about disclosure of any self-reported inappropriate behaviors to the department's administration. So while veracity could still be considered an issue, it is less of a threat given that officers did not reveal information regarding their own improper behavior.

Practically, there is a different set of considerations that must be addressed. When thinking about generalizing this research to other police departments in the U.S. and the U.K., several limitations are present. There are also concerns regarding the differences between the two departments. While these limitations do not fatally flaw the study, they must be taken into consideration.

First, the London Metropolitan Police may not be representative of the police in the U.K. The MET is the largest police organization in the U.K. with over 30,000 officers. A department of this size serving a population of over eight million residents brings different tactical, strategic, and organizational concerns than in many of the smaller, more rural departments in the U.K. London is also the most diverse city in the U.K. with both residents and tourists, and other departments may not share the views of disrespect and the experiences with disrespect that officers in London do. As such, what officers in London deem to be disrespectful may not carry over to other, smaller departments in the U.K. Replication in a variety of U.K. police departments would be appropriate.

The same holds true for officers in the U.S. Only one mid-sized southeastern city department was sampled for this study and within that department, only 79 officers responded to the survey instrument. This would allow one to generalize to similar departments but without more study participants, those generalizations would need to be made with caution.

Cross-nationally, there is also a concern regarding the comparability of these departments as they are different in many respects. The departments are most noticeably different in size but also in organizational structure. They differ with the citizenry they serve with London officers serving a much more diverse population of both tourists and residents. Even with these differences, both departments function in a similar manner and the officers in the sample are alike in many respects. Moreover, the results revealed patterns consistent to officers in both departments which would suggest these differences may not have significantly influenced the results.

Avenues for Future Research

This study marks the first effort that focuses primarily on officers' perceptions of citizen disrespect, and as noted above, it fills a needed gap in the research. In attempts to gain better understandings of police behavior(s), knowing how officers see and interpret behaviors is crucial. The direct contributions notwithstanding, first efforts often breed more questions than answers and this research is no exception.

The following section will outline possible avenues for future research in this area.

First, this survey did not ask officers to address how they might respond to citizen disrespect when they encounter it. Physical and verbal affronts or attacks from citizens can lead to aggressive responses from officers (Birkbeck and LaFree, 1993; Dunham and Alpert, 2009) and levels of restraint in the face of these attacks can vary. Officers may choose to deflect or de-escalate where possible/practical but others may choose to punish the transgressor. These punishments can be formal or informal and may include verbal and/or physical responses, such as verbal reprimands, arrests, or uses of force.

Utilizing an officer-driven conceptualization of disrespect in this type of explanatory study is the logical follow-up to the present one. In the U.S., an officer-based conceptualization of disrespect should lead to increased levels of validity and reliability and as these levels increase, a better understanding of police reactions to disrespect will follow. In the U.K., this study could be a valuable starting point for research on disrespect and police decision making.

Second, future research can also work to replicate these results and move beyond the two departments assessed here. In the U.S., only one mid-sized city police department in the southeast was sampled. It would be beneficial to study departments of different size and in different regions to see if their perceptions were similar to the current sample. In the U.K., only the London Metropolitan Police was sampled. In relation to the organizational strength and size, the MET is clearly the outlier among England's police departments. The MET employs almost one-fifth of all police officers among the 43 departments in both England and Wales (Bullock, 2008).[61] It would be valuable to seek out smaller departments in other cities and in rural England in an effort to determine if officers in the MET have similar perceptions of and experiences with disrespect.

Thinking about police more generally, this research works toward answering the question of whether a cop is a cop, both within a single country and among different countries. Future research should move beyond the borders of England and the U.S. and should seek out

---

[61] As of September 30, 2007, there were 141,731 full time police officers in England and Wales.

countries with wholly different sets of norms. For instance, it would be interesting to replicate this study in countries such as Japan or China given the stark contrast in cultures and norms. Certainly, understanding how officers define disrespect and how often they experience disrespect can be beneficial to those departments and the citizenry they serve in addition to the comparative benefit. Moreover, these types of studies could continue to assess the effect of culture on police perceptions, experiences, and behaviors.

Given the increasing focus on community policing and MET's commitment to hiring PCSO's, a comparative study among London's sworn police officers and PCSO's could be undertaken as well. From 2006 to 2007, there was an 80% increase in the number of PCSO's in the MET (Bullock, 2008), evidence of a commitment to bridging the gap between the community and police. Compared with over 30,000 police officers, the MET now employs over 15,000 PCSO's. PCSO's are highly visible and the encounters they have with the public are more voluntary in nature. As such, it would be beneficial to understand their experiences and how they compare to sworn police officers in the MET.

Thinking more about police in non-law enforcement situations, no research has focused on the prevalence of disrespect in voluntary encounters in either the U.S. or U.K. Including this one, all studies have focused on police behavior in law enforcement-related, involuntary police encounters. This is understandable given the need to know how and why police act the way they do in these encounters but thinking about the shift toward a more community oriented police mission (coupled with crime fighting), it would be valuable to learn about citizen disrespect in situations other than arrest or investigatory ones. If police are experiencing disrespect when walking down the street, patrolling in a car or on a bicycle, or in voluntary face-to-face encounters, it could signify a deeper dislike for police or more substantial problems in the police-citizen relationship.

Along similar lines, are officers more aware of disrespectful behaviors or does their threshold of disrespect lower when other officers are present? Past research has indicated that officers may change their behavior in situations where other officers or supervisors are present (Worden, 1995; Brooke, 2001; Dai et al., 2011). Officers may feel the need to 'save face' in the presence of others and if this is the case, then disrespect may be more likely to be perceived when officers are acting together. Similarly, it would be interesting to know if the perception of disrespect varied in different types of encounters where more than one officer or where supervisor(s) were present.

Additionally, very few studies have been completed that have examined the behaviors of off duty officers. This is certainly understandable given that off duty officers rarely become involved in law enforcement-related encounters. While a study exploring their own behaviors off duty might be less valuable, a study investigating their experiences with disrespect while off duty would be. Similar to this research, a study of this kind could focus on how often they perceive disrespect, which behaviors they are experiencing, and in what context or situation they are experiencing them in. Moreover, given the strength of police subculture in both countries and the probability that police officers will associate with other officers off duty, it would be interesting to know if they feel that they are disrespected by citizens who recognize them as police officers - while in a group.

Finally, this research revealed interesting results in relation to education, experience, and traffic stops that could be revisited in future studies. It was found that education and experience were positively related to disrespect in most of the equations. It would be interesting to see if these relationships held up in other research sites and a study of this kind could shed light upon the question of why educated officers respond less negatively to disrespect (see Worden, 1995) if they experience it more often.

In relation to traffic stops, it was striking to find that U.K. officers experienced disrespect 'often' with traffic suspects at a rate almost six times that of U.S. officers. Why do traffic stops in the U.K. yield so much more disrespect, from both suspects and those cited? In the U.K., a study concentrating on this specific aspect could yield information that assist officers in de-escalating potentially volatile traffic stops.

In all, it is clear that contributions were made with this study but as noted above, this is simply the beginning. There are avenues for future research that could benefit departments in the two countries studied and in departments worldwide. With the over-reaching goal of understanding police actions and reactions in police-citizen encounters, the opportunities to improve and move beyond the present research are clear.

Conclusion

As this research has demonstrated, behaviors that officers themselves determine to be disrespectful differ from how previous inquiries have conceptualized disrespect. In short, their definition is more inclusive, includes illegal behaviors, ones that occur prior to the face-to face interaction, and ones that are not necessarily hostile or antagonistic. It is also clear that a degree of consistency exists among officers in both departments as to what they believe to be disrespectful, implying that the similarities in police subculture may play a more significant role with police perceptions than the country's culture. More importantly, these results indicate that Klinger and Worden were both on point in their assertions regarding the inclusion of criminal conduct in the conceptualization of disrespect. Since illegal behaviors were still found to be disrespectful by the majority of officers, the effects should be parsed out rather than excluded. Years of research and Klinger's comments notwithstanding, work in this area and this study should still be considered preliminary.

Thinking in practical terms, the implications are clear. Disrespectful behavior that falls short of criminality should never be considered justification for a formal or informal sanction. Moreover, officers' decisions to sanction based on disrespectful behaviors that are illegal should be both formal (i.e. arrest) and proportional to that disrespectful behavior. In other words, when confronted by disrespectful behaviors that are also illegal, officers should use reasonable force only when necessary and arrest only when warranted.

If one of the goals of police research is to understand how and why officers choose to act and react the way they do, then it is imperative to recognize the value of how they perceive and interpret the behaviors of citizens during these interactions. This study allows officers and police administrations in both departments to do just that. With an increased awareness in departments and by individual officers, the hope remains that police-citizen encounters in both countries can become more civil, that officers will make stronger efforts at de-escalation, and that they will exercise restraint in the face of citizen disrespect.

APPENDIX I: Oak Ridge Police Officer Survey Form

Instructions: Thank you for participating in this study. Please follow the directions that are listed before each question. The instructions for each question will be in this font and will be bolded. The questions themselves will be in this font and will not be bolded.

1a. In your own words, how would you describe or define citizen disrespect?

1b. Please think for a minute and list as many citizen behaviors as you can that you find to be disrespectful. These can be any verbal behaviors or actions, gestures, or physical behaviors. Try to list at least 10 behaviors. **Please do not go forward into this survey until you have completed these two questions.**

List of behaviors (and any explanation if needed)
1.
2.
3.
4.
5.
6.
7.
8.
9.
10.

Other Behaviors:

2. Please rip off the last page in this packet and look at list A**. I'm going to ask you a few questions focusing on how often you experience citizen disrespect in encounters on a general basis. Please place the number associated with your response into the box below.**

Responses:
[1] = Often   [2] = Sometimes   [3] = Rarely   [4] = Never
[5] = Does not apply
[8] = Don't know/no opinion

2a. Looking at list A, please tell me how often you have experienced disrespectful suspects in these types of encounters. **Please place your answers in the column 2a for each type of encounter.**

2b. Now I want you to think about your experiences with citizens who you have arrested. Please tell me how often you have experienced disrespect from citizens in these types of encounters that you have just arrested. **Please place your answers in the column 2b for each type of encounter.**

2c. Now I want you to think about your experiences with crime victims. Please tell me how often you have experienced crime victims in these types of encounters who have been disrespectful toward you. **Please place your answers in the column 2c for each type of encounter.**

	2a. Suspects	2b. Arrestees	2c. Crime victims
Traffic stops – non DUI			Does not apply
Traffic stops - DUI			Does not apply
Drug offenses			Does not apply
Non serious criminal offenses (i.e. trespass, larceny...)			
Serious criminal offenses (robbery, rape...)			

**Now I want you to think about disrespectful actions more
specifically. The next several questions will focus on specific
behaviors.**

3a. Please indicate <u>all behaviors you deem to be disrespectful</u> toward
you as a police officer. **Please place check marks in columns 3a for
all the behaviors you personally find to be disrespectful. If there
are behaviors that you believe to be disrespectful that are not listed
here, please indicate them below.**

3b. What behaviors do you believe <u>other officers</u> deem to be
disrespectful? **Please place check marks in columns 3b for all
behaviors you think other police officers would deem disrespectful.**

	self 3a.	others 3b.		self 3a.	others 3b.
[1] Impolite or discourteous			[12] Makes obscene gesture to P.O.		
[2] Verbally antagonistic			[13] Spits toward P.O.		
[3] Ignores requests/commands			[14] Takes a defensive/ aggressive stance		
[4] Argues/denies accusations			[15] Physically resists arrest/ detention		
[5] Curses/uses profanity			[16] Assaults P.O.		
[6] Makes derogatory statement to P.O.			[17] Attempts escape - flees/runs		
[10] Makes a physical threat to P.O.			[18] Pursuit		
[11] Other verbal			[19] Other Physical		
1.			1.		
2.			2.		
3.			3.		

4a. Please list what you feel are the two <u>most common</u> displays of disrespect from citizens that <u>you</u> have personally experienced. **Please list the most common behavior first and the second most common after that.**

4b. Please list what you feel are the two <u>least common</u> displays of disrespect from citizens that <u>you</u> have personally experienced. **Please list the least common behavior first and the second least common after that.**

4c. Please list what you feel are the two <u>most common</u> displays of disrespect from citizens that you believe <u>other officers</u> have personally experienced. **Please list the most common behavior first and the second most common after that.**

4d. Please list what you feel are the two <u>least common</u> displays of disrespect from citizens that you believe <u>other officers</u> have personally experienced. **Please list the least common behavior first and the second least common after that.**

5a. In your opinion, of all the behaviors that you deem to be disrespectful, which ones do <u>you</u> find to be the <u>most offensive</u> to you personally? **Please list the most offensive behavior first and the second most offensive after that.**

5b. In your opinion, of all the behaviors on this list, which do you believe <u>other officers</u> find to be the <u>most offensive</u>? Please list the two behaviors. **Please list the most offensive behavior first and the second most offensive after that.**

6a. Think about a situation where you're investigating a low level theft and are interviewing a suspect. At this point in the investigation, you *do not* have enough evidence to arrest for the theft. If you initially perceive that the citizen is being <u>verbally</u> disrespectful toward you (without violating any laws), how would you respond <u>at that specific point</u>? **[place check mark in the appropriate box under column 6a]**

6b. If that same citizen continued to be verbally disrespectful toward you throughout that encounter, how would you respond? **[place check mark in the appropriate box under column 6b]**

7a. Think about the same situation where you're investigating a low level theft and are interviewing a suspect. At this point in the investigation however, you *do not* have enough evidence to arrest for the theft. If you initially perceive that the citizen is being <u>verbally</u> disrespectful toward you (without violating any laws), how would you respond <u>at that specific point</u>? **[place check mark in the appropriate box under column 7a.]**

7b. If that same citizen continued to be verbally disrespectful toward you throughout that encounter, how would you respond? **[place check mark in the appropriate box under column 7b]**

	6a.	6b.	7a.	7b.
[1] Behavior would not change				
[2] Tone becomes more authoritative				
[3] Issue request or command to citizen to change their behavior				
[4] Threaten to use physical force				
[5] Physically restrain citizen				
[6] Use physical force > restraint				
[10] Threaten to arrest				
[11] Arrest citizen				
[7] Other **(write in response below)**				

8. Think more generally about verbal disrespect for a moment. When at an encounter with a citizen, what <u>verbal</u> cues *initially* indicate or give you the first clue that this citizen is showing disrespect? So rather than asking about the most common behaviors you see, I'm asking which verbally disrespectful behavior is usually the <u>first one</u> you see. **[place check mark in the appropriate box under columns marked 'response.]**

	Response ↓		Response ↓
[1] Impolite or discourteous		[6] Derogatory statement	
[2] Verbally antagonistic		[11] Verbal physical threat	
[3] Ignores requests or commands		[7] Other - **write in response below**	
[4] Argues/denies accusations			
[5] Curses/uses profanity			

9a. Going back to that same situation where you're investigating a low level theft and are interviewing a suspect. At this point in the investigation, you *do not* have enough evidence to arrest for the theft. If you initially perceive that the citizen is being physically disrespectful (actual physical behaviors or gestures rather than words) toward you (without violating any laws), how would you respond at that specific point? **[place check mark in the appropriate box under column 9a]**

9b. If that same citizen continued to be physically disrespectful toward you throughout the encounter, how would you respond? **[place check mark in the appropriate box under column 9b]**

10a. Think about the same theft investigation but at this point in the investigation however, you *do* have enough evidence to arrest for the theft. If you initially perceive that the citizen is being physically disrespectful toward you (without violating any laws), how would you respond at that specific point? **[place check mark in the appropriate box under column 10a]**

10b. If that same citizen continued to be physically disrespectful toward you throughout the encounter, how would you respond? **[place check mark in the appropriate box under column 10b]**

	9a.	9b.	10a.	10b.
[1] Behavior would not change				
[2] Tone becomes more authoritative				
[3] Issue request or command to citizen to change their behavior				
[4] Threaten to use physical force				
[5] Physically restrain citizen				
[6] Use physical force > restraint				
[10] Threaten to arrest				
[11] Arrest citizen				
[7] Other **(write in response below)**				

11. Think more generally about physical disrespectful for a moment. When at an encounter with a citizen, what <u>physical</u> behaviors or gestures *initially* indicate or give you the first clue that this citizen is showing disrespect? So again, rather than asking about the most common behaviors you see, I'm asking which disrespectful behavior is usually the <u>first one</u> you see. **[place check mark in the appropriate box under column marked 'response.]**

	Response ↓		Response ↓
[3] Ignores commands to move		[17] Attempts escape	
[12] Makes obscene gesture		[18] Pursuit	
[13] Spits towards officer		[19] Other Physical **(write in response below)**	
[14] Takes a defensive/aggressive			

stance			
[15] Physically resists arrest/detention			
[16] Assaults officer			

12a. How often have you <u>actually experienced</u> disrespect from citizens in these specific types of encounters? **Please place the number of the response in column 12a below <u>for each</u> type of encounter**

[1] = Often   [2] = Sometimes   [3] = Rarely   [4] = Never
[8] = Don't know

12b. Could you describe the most common type of disrespect you've encountered in each of the below encounters. **Please place the number of the response in column 12b below <u>for each</u> type of encounter.**

12c. In your experience as a police officer, have you ever received a _____ call *where* (prior to arrival), you <u>anticipated</u> that you would encounter a disrespectful citizen? **Please place the number of the response in column 12c below <u>for each</u> type of encounter.**

1] = yes   [2] = no   [8] = don't know

12d. What was it that made you anticipate disrespect in this specific type of encounter? **Please place the number of the response in column 12d below <u>for each</u> type of encounter**

   [1] = experienced disrespect in same type of encounter in past
   [2] = experienced disrespect from exact same citizen in past
   [3] = experienced disrespect in same neighborhood in past
   [4] = not applicable
   [7] = other
   [8] = don't know

	12a. experienced	12b. most common	12c. anticipated	12d. reason for anticipation
Encounter Type	1 = often 2 = sometime 3 = rarely 4 = never 8 = don't know	1-imp 12-obscene 2-V.A. 13-spit 3-ignore 14-def st. 4-arg/den 15-resist 5-profan 16-assault 6-derog 17-escape 7-other 18-pursuit 10-threat	1=yes 2=no 8=don't know	1=exp. - same enc. 2=exp. - same citizen 3=exp. - same neigh. 4=N/A 7=other 8=don't know
Domestic Disputes				
Violent Crime Calls				
Non-serious Crime Calls				
Drug Crime Calls				
Drunk and Disorderly				
Suspicious Persons				

Call for service/assistance				
Pursuits				
Traffic stops- DUI				
Traffic stops- Non DUI				

13. Based on your experience as a police officer in this city, have you gone into or been called into different police divisions in the city where you anticipated that generally, citizens would exhibit less respect for your authority? **Please place the number of the response in column 13 below.**

[1] = anticipate less respect   [2] = anticipate respect
[3] = no expectation   [7] = other
[8] = don't know, no opinion

Division	**13. Response** ↓
Eastern Division	
Western Division	
Southern Division	
Central Division	

Here are some statements about police work generally. For each one, please state the response that best indicates your opinion. The responses are as follows:

[1] agree strongly   [2] agree somewhat
[3] disagree somewhat   [4] disagree strongly
[5] no opinion   [7] other   [8] don't know

14. _____ A good patrol officer is one who patrols aggressively by stopping cars, checking out people, running license checks, and so forth.

15. _____ Police officers are distrustful of most citizens

16. _____ Police officers have reason to be distrustful of most citizens.

17. _____ Assisting citizens is just as important as enforcing the law.

18. _____ The majority of officers in your department believe that voice commands are uses of force.

19. Compared to officers in your borough/station, do you make? **Please place a check mark next to your response below.**

_____ substantially more arrests [1]
_____ more arrests [2]
_____ about the same amount of arrests [3]
_____ less arrests [4]
_____ substantially less arrests [5]

I just have a few questions about your background and you're done.

20. _____ In which division have you had the most shift assignment in the past six months?

[1] = Eastern Division
[2] = Western Division
[3] = Central Division
[4] = Southern Division
[5] = Other - Please list here _____

21. _____ How many total years have you worked as a police officer (with the Oak Ridge Police)?

22. _____ How many total years have you worked as a police officer (in all departments that you have worked for)?

23. _____ How many years of education do you have?
  [1] = high school diploma
  [2] = < 2 years college
  [3] = < 4 years college
  [4] = 4 or > years college

24. What is your age? _____

25. What is your race?
  [1] Black_____
  [2] White_____
  [3] Hispanic_____
  [7] Other **[please write in here]**

_____

26. What is your gender?
  [1] Male_____
  [2]Female_____

27. What is your ethnicity or ethnic background?

_____

Thank you for taking the time to complete this survey.

===

List A

Categories	Responses
1. Traffic stops – non DUI	1 - Often
2. Traffic stops - DUI	2.- Sometimes
3. Drug offenses	3.- Rarely
3. Non serious criminal offenses	4.- Never
(i.e. trespass, larceny..)	
4. Serious criminal offenses (robbery, rape..)	8.- Don't know or no opinion

List B

1. Impolite or discourteous
2. Verbally antagonistic
3. Ignores requests/commands
4. Argues or denies accusations
5. Curses/uses profanity
6. Makes derogatory statement
7. Makes a physical threat
8. Makes obscene gesture
9. Spits toward officer
10. Takes a defensive/aggressive stance
10. Physically resists arrest or detention
12. Assaults officer
13. Attempts escape - runs/flees
14. Pursuit
15. Other physical

List C

1. Domestic disputes
2. Violent crime calls (i.e. robbery, rape)
3. Non-serious crime calls (i.e. trespass, larceny)
4. Drug crime calls
5. Drunk + disorderly
6. Suspicious persons
7. Calls for service/assistance
8. Pursuits
9. Traffic stops – non DUI
10. DUI stops

APPENDIX II: MET Police Officer Survey Form

Instructions: **Thank you so much for participating in this study. Please follow the directions that are listed before each question. The instructions for each question will be in this font and will be bolded.** The questions will be in this font and will not be bolded.

1a. In your own words, how would you describe or define citizen disrespect?

1b. Please think for a minute and list as many citizen behaviors as you can that you find to be disrespectful. These can be any verbal behaviors or actions, gestures, or physical behaviors. Try to list at least 10 behaviors. Please do not go forward into this survey until you have completed these two questions.

List of behaviors (and any explanation if needed)
1.
2.
3.
4.
5.
6.
7.
8.
9.
10.

Other Behaviors:

2. Please rip off the last page in this packet and look at list A. I'm going to ask you a few questions focusing on how often you experience citizen disrespect in encounters on a general basis. Please place the number associated with your response into the box below.
Responses:
[1] = Often   [2] = Sometimes   [3] = Rarely   [4] = Never
[5] = Does not apply
[8] = Don't know/no opinion

2a. Looking at list A, please tell me how often you have experienced disrespectful suspects in these types of encounters. **Please place your answers in the column 2a for each type of encounter.**

2b. Now I want you to think about your experiences with citizens who you have placed into custody. Please tell me how often you have experienced disrespect from citizens in these types of encounters that you have just placed into custody **Please place your answers in the column 2b for each type of encounter.**

2c. Now I want you to think about your experiences with crime victims. Please tell me how often you have experienced crime victims in these types of encounters who have been disrespectful toward you. **Please place your answers in the column 2c for each type of encounter.**

	2a. Suspects	2b. Arrestees	2c. Crime victims
Traffic stops – non Drink Drive			Does not apply
Traffic stops - Drink Drive			Does not apply
Drug offenses			Does not apply
Non serious criminal offenses (i.e. trespass, larceny...)			
Serious criminal offenses (robbery, rape...)			

Now I want you to think about disrespectful actions more specifically. The next several questions will focus on specific behaviors. Please look at list B when answering these questions.

3a. Please indicate <u>all behaviors you deem to be disrespectful</u> toward you as a police officer. **Please place check marks in columns 3a for all the behaviors you find to be disrespectful. If there are behaviors that you find to be disrespectful that are not listed here, please indicate them below.**

3c. What behaviors do you believe <u>other officers</u> deem to be disrespectful? **Please place check marks in columns 3b for all behaviors you think other police officers would deem disrespectful.**

	self	others		self	others
	3a.	**3c.**		**3a.**	**3c.**
[1] Impolite or discourteous			[12] Makes obscene gesture to P.O.		
[2] Verbally antagonistic			[13] Spits toward P.O.		
[3] Ignores requests/commands			[14] Takes a defensive/aggressive stance		
[4] Argues/denies accusations			[15] Physically resists arrest/detention		
[5] Curses/uses profanity			[16] Assaults P.O.		
[6] Makes derogatory statement to P.O.			[17] Attempts escape - flees/runs		
[10] Makes a physical threat to P.O.			[18] Pursuit		
[11] Other verbal			[19] Other Physical		
1.			1.		
2.			2.		
3.			3.		

4a. Please list what you feel are the two <u>most common</u> displays of disrespect from citizens that <u>you</u> have personally experienced. **Please list the most common behavior first and the second most common after that.**

4b. Please list what you feel are the two <u>least common</u> displays of disrespect from citizens that <u>you</u> have personally experienced. **Please list the least common behavior first and the second least common after that.**

4c. Please list what you feel are the two <u>most common</u> displays of disrespect from citizens that you believe <u>other officers</u> have personally experienced. **Please list the most common behavior first and the second most common after that.**

4d. Please list what you feel are the two <u>least common</u> displays of disrespect from citizens that you believe <u>other officers</u> have personally experienced. **Please list the least common behavior first and the second least common after that.**

5a. In your opinion, of all the behaviors that you deem to be disrespectful, which ones <u>you</u> find to be the <u>most offensive</u> to you personally? **Please list the most offensive behavior first and the second most offensive after that.**

5b. In your opinion, of all the behaviors on this list, which do you believe <u>other officers</u> find to be the <u>most offensive</u>? Please list the two behaviors. **Please list the most offensive behavior first and the second most offensive after that.**

6a. Think about a situation where you're investigating a low level theft and are interviewing a suspect. At this point in the investigation, you *do not* have enough evidence to arrest for the theft. If you initially perceive that the citizen is being <u>verbally</u> disrespectful toward you (without violating any laws), how would you respond <u>at that specific point</u>? **[place check mark in the appropriate box under column 6a]**

6b. If that same citizen continued to be verbally disrespectful toward you throughout that encounter, how would you respond? **[place check mark in the appropriate box under column 6b]**

7a. Think about the same situation where you're investigating a low level theft and are interviewing a suspect. At this point in the investigation however, you _do_ have enough evidence to arrest for the theft. If you initially perceive that the citizen is being verbally disrespectful toward you (without violating any laws), how would you respond at that specific point? **[place check mark in the appropriate box under column 7a.]**

7b. If that same citizen continued to be verbally disrespectful toward you throughout that encounter, how would you respond? **[place check mark in the appropriate box under column 7b]**

	6a.	6b.	7a.	7b.
[1] Behavior would not change				
[2] Tone becomes more authoritative				
[3] Issue request or command to citizen to change their behavior				
[4] Threaten to use physical force				
[5] Physically restrain citizen				
[6] Use physical force > restraint				
[10] Threaten to arrest				
[11] Arrest citizen				
[7] Other **(write in response below)**				

8. Think more generally about verbal disrespect for a moment. When at an encounter with a citizen, what verbal cues *initially* indicate or give you the first clue that this citizen is showing disrespect? So rather than asking about the most common behaviors you see, I'm asking which verbally disrespectful behavior is usually the first one you see. **[place check mark in the appropriate box under column marked 'response.]**

	Response ↓		Response ↓
[1] Impolite or discourteous		[6] Derogatory statement	
[2] Verbally antagonistic		[11] Verbal physical threat	
[3] Ignores requests or commands		[7] Other - **write in response below**	
[4] Argues/denies accusations			
[5] Curses/uses profanity			

9a. Going back to that same situation where you're investigating a low level theft and are interviewing a suspect. At this point in the investigation, you *do not* have enough evidence to arrest for the theft. If you initially perceive that the citizen is being <u>physically</u> disrespectful (actual physical behaviors or gestures rather than words) toward you (without violating any laws), how would you respond <u>at that specific point</u>? [place check mark in the appropriate box under column 9a]

9b. If that same citizen continued to be physically disrespectful toward you throughout the encounter, how would you respond? [place check mark in the appropriate box under column 9b]

10a. Think about the same theft investigation but at this point in the investigation however, you *do* have enough evidence to arrest for the theft. If you initially perceive that the citizen is being <u>physically</u> disrespectful toward you (without violating any laws), how would you respond <u>at that specific point</u>? [place check mark in the appropriate box under column 10a]

10b. If that same citizen continued to be physically disrespectful toward you throughout the encounter, how would you respond? [place check mark in the appropriate box under column 10b]

	9a.	9b.	10a.	10b.
[1] Behavior would not change				
[2] Tone becomes more authoritative				
[3] Issue request or command to citizen to change their behavior				
[4] Threaten to use physical force				
[5] Physically restrain citizen				
[6] Use physical force > restraint				
[10] Threaten to arrest				
[11] Arrest citizen				
[7] Other (write in response below)				

11. Think more generally about physical disrespectful for a moment. When at an encounter with a citizen, what <u>physical</u> behaviors or gestures *initially* indicate or give you the first clue that this citizen is showing disrespect? So again, rather than asking about the most common behaviors you see, I'm asking which disrespectful behavior is usually the <u>first one</u> you see. **[place check mark in the appropriate box under column marked 'response.]**

	Response ↓		Response ↓
[3] Ignores commands to move		[17] Attempts escape	
[12] Makes obscene gesture		[18] Pursuit	
[13] Spits towards officer		[19] Other Physical (write in response below)	
[14] Takes a defensive/ aggressive stance			
[15] Physically resists arrest/detention			
[16] Assaults officer			

Please take a look at list C. I'm going to ask you a few questions relative to that list. Please place the number of the response under the column for that question.

12a. How often have you <u>actually experienced</u> disrespect from citizens in these specific types of encounters? **Please place the number of the response in column 12a below_for each type of encounter**

[1] = Often   [2] = Sometimes   [3] = Rarely   [4]   =   Never
[8] = Don't know

12b. Could you describe the most common types of disrespect you've encountered in each of the below encounters. **Please refer back to List B if you need to. Please place the number of the response in column 12b below for each type of encounter.**

12c. In your experience as a police officer, have you ever received a _____ call *where* (prior to arrival), you begin to <u>anticipate</u> that you will encounter a disrespectful citizen? **Please place the number of the response in column 12c below_for each type of encounter.**

[1] = yes   [2] = no   [8] = don't know

12d. What was it that made you anticipate disrespect in this specific type of encounter? **Please place the number of the response in column 12d below_for each type of encounter**

[1] = experienced disrespect in same type of encounter in past
[2] = experienced disrespect from exact same citizen in past
[3] = experienced disrespect in same neighborhood in past
[4] = not applicable
[7] = other
[8] = don't know

Encounter Type	12a. experienced	12b. 1st most common	12c. anticipated	12d. reason for anticipation
	1 = often 2 = some-times 3 = rarely 4 = never 8 = don't know	1-imp 12-obscene 2-V.A. 13-spit 3-ignor 14-def st. 4-arg/den 15-resist 5-prof 16-assault 6-derog 17-escape 7-other 18-pursuit 10-threat	1=yes 2=no 8=don't know	1=exp. - same enc. 2=exp. - same citizen 3=exp. - same neigh. 4=N/A 7=other 8=don't know
Domestic Disputes				
Violent Crime Calls				
Non-serious Crime Calls				
Drug Crime Calls				
Drunk and Disorderly				
Suspicious Persons				

Encounter Type	12a. experienced	12b. 1st most common	12c. anticipated	12d. reason for anticipation
	1 = often 2 = some-times 3 = rarely 4 = never 8 = don't know	1-imp 12-obscene 2-V.A. 13-spit 3-ignor 14-def st. 4-arg/den 15-resist 5-prof 16-assault 6-derog 17-escape 7-other 18-pursuit 10-threat	1=yes 2=no 8=don't know	1=exp. - same enc. 2=exp. - same citizen 3=exp. - same neigh. 4=N/A 7=other 8=don't know
Call for service/assistance				
Pursuits				
Traffic stops- Drink Drive				
Traffic stops- Non Drink Drive				

Just about there - just a few more quick questions and you'll be done.

13. Based on your experience as a police officer in this city, have you gone into or been called into different police boroughs in the city where you anticipated that generally, citizens would exhibit less respect for your authority? **Please place the number of the response in column 13 below.**

[1] = anticipate less respect   [2] = anticipate respect
[3] = no expectation   [7] = other
[8] = don't know, no opinion

Borough	13. Response ↓
Kensington	
Chelsea	
Notting Hill	
Other - please write in below	

Here are some statements about police work generally. For each one, please state the response that best indicates your opinion. The responses are as follows:

[1] agree strongly   [2] agree somewhat   [3] disagree somewhat
[4] disagree strongly [5] no opinion   [7] other
[8]don't know

14. _____ A good patrol officer is one who patrols aggressively by stopping cars, checking out people, running license checks, and so forth.

15. _____ Police officers are distrustful of most citizens

16. _____ Police officers have reason to be distrustful of most citizens.

17. _____ Assisting citizens is just as important as enforcing the law.

18. _____ The majority of officers in your department believe that voice commands are uses of force.

OK, I have one more question about police work in general.

19. Compared to officers in your borough/station, do you make? **Please place a check mark next to your response below.**

_____ substantially more arrests [1]
_____ more arrests [2]
_____ about the same amount of arrests [3]
_____ less arrests [4]
_____ substantially less arrests [5]

I just have a few questions about your background and you're done.

20. _____ Which borough have you had the most shift assignment in the past six months?

[1] = Kensington
[2] = Chelsea
[3] = Notting Hill
[4] = Other - Please list here _____

21. _____ How many total years have you worked as a police officer (with the MET police)?

22. _____ How many total years have you worked as a police officer (in all departments that you have worked for)?

23. _____ How many years of education do you have?
   [1] = high school diploma
   [2] = < 2 years college
   [3] = < 4 years college
   [4] = 4 or > years college

24. What is your age? _____

25. What is your race?
   [1] = Black_____
   [2] = White_____
   [3] = Hispanic_____
   [7] = Other **[please write in here]** _____

26. What is your gender?
   [1] = Male_____
   [2] = Female_____

27. What is your ethnicity or ethnic background? _____ _____

28. What is your current position?
   [1]= Police Officer
   [2] = Police Community Support Officer
   [3] = Special Constable
   [7] = Other **[please write in here]** _____

29. What is your current assignment?
   [1] = Foot patrol
   [2] = Vehicle patrol
   [3] = Vehicle patrol - Firearms
   [7] = Other **[please write in here]** _____

List A

Categories	Responses

1. Traffic stops – non Drink Drive   1 - Often
2. Traffic stops - Drink Drive   2.- Sometimes
3. Drug offenses   3.- Rarely
3. Non serious criminal offenses   4.- Never
     (i.e. trespass, larceny..)
4. Serious criminal offenses   8.-Don't know or no opinion
     (robbery, rape..)

List B

1. Impolite or discourteous
2. Verbally antagonistic
3. Ignores requests/commands
4. Argues or denies accusations
5. Curses/uses profanity
6. Makes derogatory statement
7. Makes a physical threat
8. Makes obscene gesture
9. Spits toward officer
10. Takes a defensive/aggressive stance
10. Physically resists arrest or detention
12. Assaults officer
13. Attempts escape - runs/flees
14. Pursuit
15. Other physical

List C

1. Domestic disputes
2. Violent crime calls (i.e. robbery, rape)
3. Non-serious crime calls (i.e. trespass, larceny)
4. Drug crime calls
5. Drunk + disorderly

6. Suspicious persons
7. Calls for service/assistance
8. Pursuits
9. Traffic stops – non Drink Drive
10. Drink Drive stops

Appendix IIIa. Multivariate Models Estimating Definitional Inclusivity: Quantitative Verbal Disrespect

Dependent Variables	Model 1 Impoliteness β (SE)	Model 2 Verbal Antagonism β (SE)	Model 3 Ignores Commands β (SE)	Model 4 Denies Accusations β (SE)
Constant	.566 (.166)	1.036 (.165)	.929 (.116)	1.191 (.252)
Independent Variable				
U.K Officers	.149 (.049)	-.236* (.049)	-.194 (.034)	-.195 (.075)
Control Variables				
White	.042 (.071)	-.043 (.070)	-.164 (.049)	-.087 (.107)
Male	.153 (.071)	.210* (.071)	.502** (.049)	.143 (.108)
Education	.126 (.020)	-.058 (.020)	-.074 (.014)	-.217* (.031)
Experience	.101 (.003)	-.292* (.003)	.037 (.002)	-.172 (.005)

a. Model 1: R^2 =.054, Adjusted R^2 =.024. N=160.
b. Model 2: R^2 =.126, Adjusted R^2 =.098. N=160.
c. Model 3: R^2 =.312 Adjusted R^2 =.290 N= 160.
d. Model 4: R^2 =.093 Adjusted R^2 =.063. N= 160.
e. Effect size denoted as: *es>.20, **es>.50, ***es>.80.

Appendix IIIb. Multivariate Models Estimating Definitional Inclusivity: Qualitative Verbal Disrespect

Dependent Variables	Model 1 Impoliteness	Model 2 Verbal Antagonism	Model 3 Ignores Commands	Model 4 Denies Accusations
	β (SE)	β (SE)	β (SE)	β (SE)
Constant	.305	.643	1.239	.343
	(.283)	(.273)	(.274)	(.286)
Independent Variable				
U.K Officers	-.090	-.094	-.278*	-.143
	(.085)	(.082)	(.083)	(.086)
Control Variables				
White	.136	.062	-.122	.062
	(.119)	(.115)	(.115)	(.108)
Male	.001	-.066	.008	-.052
	(.124)	(.115)	(.120)	(.125)
Education	.038	.030	-.099	-.011
	(.035)	(.033)	(.034)	(.035)
Experience	-.185	-.062	-.079	.096
	(.006)	(.005)	(.005)	(.006)

a. Model 1: R^2 =.050, Adjusted R^2 =.020. N=164.
b. Model 2: R^2 =.023, Adjusted R^2 =-.008. N=164.
c. Model 3: R^2 =.084, Adjusted R^2 =.055. N=164.
d. Model 4: R^2 =.043, Adjusted R^2 =.013. N=164.
e. Effect size denoted as: *es>.20, **es>.50, ***es>.80.

Appendix IIIc. Multivariate Models Estimating Definitional Inclusivity: Quantitative Verbal Disrespect

Dependent Variables	Model 1 Uses Profanity β (SE)	Model 2 Derogatory Statement β (SE)	Model 3 Physical Threat β (SE)
Constant	1.060 (.234)	.862 (.112)	.962 (.102)
Independent Variable			
U.K Officers	-.048 (.069)	-.167 (.033)	-.175 (.030)
Control Variables			
White	-.110 (.100)	-.046 (.048)	-.054 (.043)
Male	-.035 (.100)	.426* (.048)	.168 (.044)
Education	.126 (.028)	-.039 (.014)	.002 (.012)
Experience	-.065 (.005)	-.124 (.002)	.064 (.002)

a. Model 1: R² =.047, Adjusted R² =.016. N=160.
b. Model 2: R² =.189, Adjusted R² =.162. N=160.
c. Model 3: R² =.066, Adjusted R² =-.036. N=160.
d. Effect size denoted as: *es>.20, **es>.50, ***es>.80.

Appendix IIId. Multivariate Models Estimating Definitional Inclusivity: Qualitative Verbal Disrespect

Dependent Variables	Model 1 Uses Profanity β (SE)	Model 2 Derogatory Statement β (SE)	Model 3 Physical Threat β (SE)	Model 4 Racial Remark β (SE)
Constant	.574 (.273)	.299 (.279)	.522 (.228)	.034 (.211)
Independent Variable				
U.K Officers	-.092 (.082)	-.133 (.084)	-.032 (.069)	-.211* (.064)
Control Variables				
White	.085 (.115)	.097 (.118)	-.006 (.096)	.029 (.089)
Male	.022 (.120)	-.069 (.122)	-.168 (.100)	.126 (.092)
Education	-.103 (.034)	.037 (.034)	-.122 (.028)	.000 (.026)
Experience	-.026 (.005)	-.104 (.006)	-.080 (.004)	.042 (.004)

a. Model 1: R² =.019, Adjusted R² =-.012. N=163.
b. Model 2: R² =.043, Adjusted R² =.012. N=164.
c. Model 3: R² =.041, Adjusted R² =.010. N=164.
d. Model 4: R² =.062, Adjusted R² =.032. N=164.
e. Effect size denoted as: *es>.20, **es>.50, ***es>.80.

Appendix IVa. Multivariate Models Estimating Definitional Inclusivity: Quantitative Physical Disrespect

Dependent Variables	Model 1 Defensive Stance β (SE)	Model 2 Resists Arrest β (SE)
Constant	1.156 (.210)	1.000 (.224)
Independent Variable		
U.K. Officers	-.491* (.062)	-.217* (.066)
Control Variables		
White	.015 (.090)	.064 (.095)
Male	-.013 (.090)	-.048 (.096)
Education	-.090 (.025)	-.133 (.027)
Experience	-.175 (.004)	-.160 (.004)

a. Model 1: R^2 =.211, Adjusted R^2 =.185. N=159.
b. Model 2: R^2 =.056, Adjusted R^2 =.025. N=160.
c. Effect size denoted as: *es>.20, **es>.50, ***es>.80.

Appendix IVb. Multivariate Models Estimating Definitional Inclusivity: Qualitative Physical Disrespect

Dependent Variables	Model 1 Spits β (SE)	Model 2 Defensive Stance β (SE)	Model 3 Resists Arrest β (SE)	Model 4 Assaults Officer β (SE)
Constant	.222 (.278)	.395 (.230)	.794 (.201)	1.000 (.288)
Independent Variable				
U.K Officers	.059 (.084)	-.090 (.069)	-.236* (.061)	-.088 (.087)
Control Variables				
White	.143 (.117)	-.093 (.097)	-.167 (.008)	-.107 (.121)
Male	.006 (.122)	.002 (.101)	-.090 (.088)	-.100 (.126)
Education	.008 (.034)	.042 (.028)	-.098 (.025)	.027 (.035)
Experience	-.042 (.005)	.029 (.005)	-.086 (.004)	-.022 (.006)

a. Model 1: R² =.026, Adjusted R² =-.005. N=163.
b. Model 2: R² =.023, Adjusted R² =-.008. N=164.
c. Model 3: R² =.094, Adjusted R² =.066. N=163.
d. Model 4: R² =.038, Adjusted R² =.008. N=163.
e. Effect size denoted as: *es>.20, **es>.50, ***es>.80.

Appendix IVc. Multivariate Models Estimating Definitional Inclusivity: Quantitative Physical Disrespect

Dependent Variables	Model 1 Attempts Escape β (SE)	Model 2 Pursuit β (SE)	Model 3 Obscene Gesture β (SE)
Constant	1.185 (.260)	1.444 (.267)	1.128 (.143)
Independent Variable			
U.K Officers	-.155 (.077)	-.440* (.079)	-.012 (.043)
Control Variables			
White	.091 (.111)	-.141 (.114)	-.067 (.061)
Male	.019 (.111)	-.074 (.114)	.033 (.061)
Education	-.103 (.031)	-.146 (.032)	-.190 (.017)
Experience	-.099 (.005)	-.036 (.005)	-.045 (.003)

a. Model 1: R^2 =.035, Adjusted R^2 =.004. N=159.
b. Model 2: R^2 =.209, Adjusted R^2 =.183. N=160.
c. Model 3: R^2 =.042, Adjusted R^2 =.011. N=160.
d. Effect size denoted as: *es>.20, **es>.50, ***es>.80.

Appendix IVd. Multivariate Models Estimating Definitional Inclusivity: Qualitative Physical Disrespect

Dependent Variables	Model 1 Attempts Escape β (SE)	Model 2 Pursuit β (SE)	Model 3 Obscene Gesture β (SE)
Constant	.036	.126	.270
	(.199)	(.097)	(.265)
Independent Variable			
U.K Officers	.085	-.109	.042
	(.060)	(.029)	(.080)
Control Variables			
White	.005	-.066	.156
	(.084)	(.041)	(.116)
Male	-.010	-.256*	-.179
	(.087)	(.042)	(.116)
Education	.105	-.029	.053
	(.024)	(.012)	(.033)
Experience	-.019	-.043	.070
	(.004)	(.002)	(.005)

a. Model 1: R^2 =.014, Adjusted R^2 =-.017. N=163.
b. Model 2: R^2 =.085, Adjusted R^2 =-.056. N=163.
c. Model 3: R^2 =.040, Adjusted R^2 =.010. N=163.
d. Effect size denoted as: *es>.20, **es>.50, ***es>.80.

References

Adams, Kenneth (1995). Measuring the prevalence of police abuse of force, in *And justice for all: understanding and controlling police abuse of force,* ed. William A. Geller and Hans Toch, 61-99, Washington, D.C.: Police Executive Research Forum.

_____ (1999). What we know about police use of force," in *Use of Force by Police: Overview of National and Local Data, Research Report,* 1-14, NIJ 176330.

Aiken, Leona and Stephen West (1991). *Multiple regression: Testing and interpreting interactions.* Thousand Oaks, CA: Sage Publications.

Anderson, Tammy and Joshua Mott (1998). Drug-related identity change: Theoretical development and empirical assessment, *Journal of Drug Issues* 28(2): 299-328.

Bartol, Anne and Curt Bartol (2004). *Introduction to forensic psychology: Research and application.* Thousand Oaks, CA: Sage.

Baruch, Yehuda (1999). Response rate in academic studies: A comparative analysis, *Human Relations* 52(4): 421-438.

Bayley, David (1979). Police function, structure, and control in Western Europe and North America: Comparative and historical studies, *Crime and Justice* 1: 109-143.

_____ (1985). *Patterns of policing: A comparative analysis.* New Brunswick, NJ: Rutgers University Press.

_____ (1988). *What works in policing.* New York, NY: Oxford University Press.

_____ (1994). *Police for the future.* New York, NY: Oxford University Press.

_____ and Egon Bittner (1984). Learning the skills of policing, *Law and Contemporary Problems* 47(4): 35-59.

Beaudoin, Marie-Nathalie and Maureen Taylor (2004). *Breaking the culture of bullying and disrespect, grades K-8: best practices and successful strategies*. Thousand Oaks, CA: Corwin Press

Bennett, Richard R. (2004). Comparative criminology and criminal justice research: The state of our knowledge, *Justice Quarterly* 21(1): 1-21.

Birkback, Christopher and Gary Lafree (1993). The situational analysis of crime and deviance, *Annual Review of Sociology* 19:113-137.

Bittner, Egon (1970). *The functions of police in modern society: A review of background factors, current practices, and possible role models.* Chevy Chase, MD: National Institute of Mental Health.

Black, Donald and Albert Reiss Jr. (1967). *Studies of crime and law enforcement in major metropolitan areas, Vol. 2: Field surveys III, section 1: Patterns of behavior in police and citizen transactions.* Washington DC: U.S. Government Printing Office.

Blood, Jeremy, Chief Inspector for Crime Prevention, London Metropolitan Police, Royal Borough of Kensington and Chelsea (2008). Personal Communication, April 3, 2008.

Blumberg, Michael (2001). Controlling police use of deadly force: Assessing two decades of progress, in *Critical issues in policing: Contemporary readings 4th*, ed. by R. Dunham and G. Alpert, 469-492, Prospect Heights, IL: Waveland.

Bowling, Ben, Alpo Parmar, and Coretta Phillips (2008). Policing minority ethnic communities, in *Handbook of policing 2nd ed.*, ed. Tim Newburn, 611-641, London: Willan.

Bradford, Ben (2011). Convergence, not divergence? Trends and trajectories in public contact and confidence with the police, *British Journal of Criminology*, 51(1): 179-200.

Brogden, Michael (1985). Stopping the people-Crime control versus social control in *Police: The constitution and community*, ed. by J. Baxter and L. Koffman, 91-110, Abingdon, Oxen: Professional Books.

Brooke, Laure Weber (2005). Police discretionary behavior: A study of style in, *Critical issues in policing: Contemporary readings 5th*, ed. by Roger Dunham and Geoffrey Alpert, 140-164, Prospect Heights, Il: Waveland Press.

Brown, Michael K. (1981). *Working the street: Police discretion and the dilemmas of reform.* New York: Russell Sage Foundation.

Bullock, Simon (2008). Policing service strength: England and Wales. *Home Office statistical bulletin,* London: Home Office.

Champion, Dean and Richard Hartley (2010). *Statistics for criminal justice and criminology, 3rd ed,* Upper Saddle River, NJ: Prentice Hall.

Charon, Joel M. (1998). *Symbolic interactionism: An introduction, an interpretation, an Integration,* Upper Saddle River, NJ: Prentice Hall.

Chevigny, Paul (1969). *Police power: Police abuses in New York City.* New York: Pantheon Books.

Clegg, Michelle and Sarah Kirwin (2006). *Police Services Strength: England and Wales, 31 March 2006,* London: Great Britain Home Office: Research Development and Statistics Directorate.

Cohen, J. (1988). *Statistical power analysis for the behavioral sciences* (2nd ed.). Hillsdale, NJ: Lawrence Earlbaum Associates.

Cordner, Gary (2005). Community policing: Elements and effects in, *Critical issues in policing: Contemporary readings 5th,* ed. by Roger Dunham and Geoffrey Alpert, 401-418, Prospect Heights, Il: Waveland Press.

Corner, Mark (2007). The EU and the roots of British skepticism, *Contemporary Review* 289(1687): 466-469.

Crawford, Adam (2008). Plural policing in the U.K.: Policing beyond the police in, *The handbook of policing 3rd ed.,* ed. Tim Newburn, 147-181, London: Willan.

_____ (2009). Governing through anti-social behavior, *British Journal of Criminology* 49: 810-831.

Dai, Mangyan, James Frank, and Ivan Sun (2011). Procedural justice during police-citizen encounters: The effects of process-based policing on citizen compliance and demeanor, *Journal of Criminal Justice* 39(2): 159-168.

Dammer, Harry and Ericka Fairchild (2006). *Comparative criminal justice systems 3rd ed.* Belmont, California: Wadsworth.

Deetz, Stanley (1982). Critical interpretive research in organizational communication, *Western Journal of Speech Communication* 46(2): 131-149.

Delsol, Rebekah and Michael Shiner (2006). Regulating stop and
    search: A challenge for police and community relations in England
    and Wales, *Critical Criminology* 14: 241-263.
Dunham, Roger and Geoffrey Alpert (2009). Officer and suspect
    demeanor: A qualitative analysis of change, *Police Quarterly*
    12(1): 6-21.
Emsley, Clive (2008). The birth and development of the police, in
    Handbook of policing 2ⁿᵈ ed, ed. Tim Newburn, 72-89, London:
    Willan.
Engel, Robin, James Sobol, and Robert Worden (2000). Further
    exploration of the demeanor hypothesis: The interaction effects of
    suspects' characteristics and demeanor on police behavior, *Justice
    Quarterly* 17(2): 235-258.
Federal Bureau of Investigation (2006). *Uniform Crime Reports.*
Felson, Richard (1993). Shame, anger, and aggression, *Social
    Psychology Quarterly* 56(4): 305-309.
Fields, Charles and Richter Moore (1996). *Comparative criminal
    justice: Traditional and nontraditional systems of law and control.*
    Prospect Heights, Il: Waveland.
Fox, Kate (2005). *Watching the English: The hidden rules of English
    behaviour.* London: Hodder and Stoughton.
Friedrich, Robert J. (1980). Police use of force: Individuals, situations,
    and organizations, *Annals of the American Academy of Political
    and Social Science* 452: 82-97.
Fyfe, James (1996). Methodology, substance, and demeanor in police
    observational research: A response to Lundman and others,
    Journal of Research in Crime and Delinquency 33(3): 337-248.
Garner, Joel, Christopher Maxwell, and Cedrick Hereaux (2002).
    Characteristics associated with the prevalence and severity of force
    used by police, *Justice Quarterly* 19 (4): 705-746.
Gertz, Marc, and Laura Myers (1992). Impediments to cross-national
    research: Problems of reliability and validity, *International Journal
    of Comparative and Applied Criminal Justice* 16(1): 57-65.
Gibbs, Carol, Edmund, McGarrell, and Mark Axelrod (2010).
    Transnational white-collar crime and risk, *Criminology and Public
    Policy*, 9(3): 543-560.
Giordano, Peggy, Steven Cernovich, and Jennifer Rudolph (2002).
    Gender, crime and desistance: Toward a theory of cognitive
    transformation, *American Journal of Sociology* 107: 990-1064.

Goffman, Erving (1961). *Encounters: Two studies in the sociology of interaction*. Indianapolis: Bobbs-Merrill.

Grant, J Douglas and Joan Grant (1995). Officer selection and the prevention of police abuse of force, in *And justice for all: Understanding and controlling police abuse of force,* ed. William A. Geller and Hans Toch, 137-150, Washington, D.C.: Police Executive Research Forum.

Herbert, Steve (2006). *Citizens, cops, and power: recognizing the limits of community*. Chicago: University of Chicago Press.

Home Office (2007). *Publications in crime - research and statistics publications*. Retrieved December 9, 2009 from http://www.homeoffice.gov.uk/publications/science-research-statistics/research-statistics/crime-research/

Jackson, Jonathan and Jason Sunshine (2007). Public confidence in policing: A neo-Durkheimian perspective, *British Journal of Criminology* 47(2): 214-233.

_____ and Ben Bradford (2009). Crime, policing, and social order: On the expressive nature of public confidence in policing, *British Journal of Sociology* 60(3): 493-521.

_____, Ben Bradford, and Elizabeth Stanko (2009). Contact and confidence: Revisiting the impact of public encounters with the police, *Policing and Society* 19(1): 20-46.

Jacobs, Bruce (1996). Crack dealers and restrictive deterrence: Identifying narcs, *Criminology* 34: 409-432.

Langworthy, Robert (1985). Wilson's theory of police behavior: A replication of constraint theory, *Justice Quarterly* 2(1): 89-98.

Lester (1995). Officer attitudes toward police use of force in *And justice for all: Understanding and controlling police abuse of force,* ed. William A. Geller and Hans Toch, 163-176, Washington, D.C.: Police Executive Research Forum.

Lewis, Richard D (1999). *When cultures collide: Managing successfully across cultures*. London, UK: Nicholas Brealey Publishing.

Lipsky, Michael (1980). *Street level bureaucracy: Dilemmas of the individuals in public service*. New York: Russell Sage.

Lundman, Richard J. (1994). Demeanor or crime: The Midwest City police-citizen encounters study, *Criminology* 32(4): 632-643.

_____ (1996). Demeanor and arrest: Additional evidence from previously unpublished data, *Journal of Research in Crime and Delinquency* 33:306-323

Macpherson, William (1999). *The Stephen Lawrence inquiry*. London: HMSO.

Maguire, E (2003). *Organizational structure in American police agencies: Context, complexity, and control*. Albany, NY: SUNY Press.

_____ and C.D. Uchida (2000). Measurement and explanation in the comparative study of American police organizations. *Criminal justice, Volume 4: Measurement and analysis of crime and justice*, ed. David Duffee. Washington, DC: National Institute of Justice.

Maguire, M and C. Corbett (1991). *A study of the police complaints system*. London: HMSO.

Manning, Peter (1977). *The social organization of policing*. Cambridge, MA: MIT Press.

Marenin, Otwin. (1997). Victimization surveys and the accuracy and reliability of official crime data in developing countries, *Journal of Criminal Justice* 25(6): 463-475.

Mastrofski, Stephen, Robert Worden, and Jeffrey Snipes (1995). Law enforcement in a time of community policing, *Criminology* 33: 539-563.

_____ , Michael Reisig, and John McCluskey (2002). Police disrespect toward the public: An encounter-based analysis, *Criminology* 40(3): 519-552.

Mawby, Rob and Alan Wright (2008). The police organization, in The *handbook of policing 2nd ed.*, ed. Tim Newburn, 224-252, London: Willan.

Maxfield, Michael and Earl Babbie (2011). *Research methods for criminal justice and criminology 6th ed.*. Belmont: Wadsworth.

McDevitt, Jack and Katrina Baum (1996). *Fight crime: Invest in kids survey of police chief views of effective crime-fighting strategies.* Center for Criminal Justice Policy Research: Northeastern University, Boston, MA.

McLaughlin, Eugene and Anja Johansen (2006). A force for change? The prospects for applying restorative justice to citizen complaints against the police in England and Wales, *British Journal of Criminology* 42: 635-653.

Metropolitan Police (2008) *London Metropolitan Police*. Retrieved February 1, 2008, from http://www.met.police.uk/.

_____ (2011). *London Metropolitan Police*. Retrieved May 18, 2011, from http://www.met.police.uk/.

Miller, Jody (1998). Up it up: Gender and the accomplishment of street robbery, *Criminology* 36: 37-66.

Miller, Joel (2010). Stop and search in England: A reformed tactic or business as usual? *British Journal of Criminology* 50(5):954-974.

_____ and Robert Davis (2008). Unpacking public attitudes to the police: Contrasting perceptions of misconduct with traditional measures of satisfaction, *International Journal of Police Science and Management* 10(1): 9-22.

Moore, Stephen (2011). Understanding and managing anti-social behaviour on public transport through value change: The considerate travel campaign, *Transport Policy* 18(1): 53-59.

National Policing Improvement Agency (2010). Retrieved May 5, 2010, from http://npia.police.uk/en/home.htm.

Newburn, Tim ed. (2008). *Handbook of policing 2nd ed.*, London: Willan.

Neyroud, Peter (2009). Squaring the circles: Research, evidence, policy-making, and police improvement in England and Wales, *Police Practice and Research* 10(5-6): 437-449.

Novak, Kenneth and Robin Shepard (2005). Disentangling the influence of suspects' demeanor and mental disorder on arrest, *Policing* 28(5): 493-512.

Office of National Statistics (2007) *Police resources: Record number of police officers in 2006*. Retrieved May 2, 2007 from http://www.statistics.gov.uk.

Office of National Statistics (2008). *The census in England and Wales*. Retrieved February 26, 2008 from http://www.statistics.gov.uk.

Olsen, Tricia, Leigh Payne, and Andrew Reiter (2010). Transitional justice in the word 1970-2007: Insights from a new data set, *Journal of Peace Research* 47(6):803-809.

Piliavin, Irving and Scott Briar (1964). Police encounters with juveniles, *American Journal of Sociology* 70: 206-214.

Pizio, William (2005). *Officers' determinations of citizen disrespect: An exploratory study,* unpublished paper, University of Albany.

Reisig, Michael, John McCluskey, Stephen Mastrofski, and William Terrill (2004). Suspect disrespect toward the police, *Justice Quarterly* 21(2): 241-268.

Reiss, Albert (1971). *The police and the public*. New Haven, CT: Yale University Press.

Riksheim, Eric and Steven Chermak. (1993). Causes of police behavior revisited, *Journal of Criminal Justice* 21:353-382.

Scott, Jan (1998). Performance culture: The return of reactive policing, *Policing and Society* 8: 269-288.

Sherman, Lawrence (1980). Causes of police behavior: The current state of quantitative research, *Journal of Research in Crime and Delinquency* 17: 69-100.

Shiner, Michael (2010). Post-Lawrence policing in England and Wales: Guilt, innocence and the defence of organizational ego, *British Journal of Criminology* 50(5): 935-953.

Skogan, Wesley (1982). Methodological issues in the measurement of crime, in *The victim in international perspective*, ed. H.J. Schneider. New York: Walter de Gruyter.

_____ and Steven Mastrofski (2002). Situational and officer-based determinants of police coercion, *Justice Quarterly* 19(2): 215-248.

Skolnick, Jerome H. (1966) *Justice without trial: Law enforcement in democratic society*. 3rd ed. Englewood Cliffs, New Jersey: MacMillan College Publishing Company.

_____ and James Fyfe (1993). *Above the law: Police and the excessive use of force*. New York: Free Press.

_____ (2008). Enduring issues of police culture and demographics, *Policing and Society* 17(1): 38-58.

Smith, D.A. and Jody R. Klein (1983). Police agency characteristics and arrest decisions in *Evaluating performance in criminal justice agencies*, ed. by Gordon Whitaker and Charles Phillips. Chicago: University of Chicago Press.

Storti, Craig (2001). *Old world, new world: Bridging cultural differences: Britain, France, Germany, and the U.S.* Boston, MA: Intercultural Press.

Sykes, R and E. Brent (1983). *Policing: A social behaviorist perspective*. New Brunswick, N.J.: Rutgers University Press.

Terrence, Allen (2005). Taking a juvenile into custody: Situational factors that influence police officers' decisions, *Journal of Sociology and Social Welfare* 32(2): 121-129.

Terrill, William, Michael Reisig (2003) Neighborhood context and the police use of force, *Journal of Research in Crime & Delinquency* 40(3): 291-321.

_____ (2005). Police use of force: A transactional approach, *Justice Quarterly* 22 (1): 107-138.

_____ and Eugene Paoline (2007). Nonarrest decision making in police-citizen encounters, *Police Quarterly* 10(3): 308-331.

Toch, Hans (1969). *Violent men: An inquiry into the psychology of violence.* Chicago: Aldine.

United States Census Bureau (2000). *2006 population estimates.* Washington: Government Printing Office.

United States Department of Justice, Bureau of Justice Statistics. Law Enforcement anagement and Administrative Statistics (2003). *U.S. population passes 290 million; Mountain and coastal states astest-growing.* Washington: Government Printing Office.

_____ (2006). *2003 Sample survey of law enforcement agencies.* Washington, DC: U.S. Dept. of Commerce, Bureau of the Census.

Van Maanen, John (1974). Working the street: A developmental view of police behavior, in *The potential for reform of criminal justice,* ed. Herbert Jacob. Beverly Hills: Sage.

_____ (1978). The Asshole, in *Policing: A view from the street,* ed. P. Manning and J. van Maanen, 228-38, Santa Monica: Goodyear.

Waddington, P.A.J. (1999a). *Policing citizens.* London: UCL Press.

_____ (1999b). Police (canteen) subculture. *British Journal of Criminology* 39(2): 287-309.

_____, Kevin Stenson, and David Don (2004). In proportion: Race, and police stop and search. *British Journal of Criminology* 44: 889-914.

_____ (2005). General commentary, in *Public order: A global perspective*, ed. Dilis Das and Allen Jiao, xii - xvii, Upper Saddle River, NJ: Pearson.

_____ and Martin Wright (2008). Police use of force, firearms, and riot control, in *Handbook of policing 2nd ed.*, ed. Tim Newburn, 465-496, London: Willan.

_____ and Martin Wright (2010). Police use of guns in unarmed countries: The United Kingdom, in *Police Use of Force: A Global Perspective,* ed. Joseph Kuhns and Johannes Knutssen, 87-94, Santa Barbara, California: Praeger.

Walters, Ian and Katie Brown (2000). Police complaints and the complainants experience, *British Journal of Criminology* 40: 617-638.

Weinberger, B (1995). *The best police in the world: An oral history of English policing from the 1930's to the 1960's*. Aldershot: Scolar.

Weisburd, David and Chester Britt (2003). *Statistics in criminal justice*, Belmont, CA: Wadsworth.

Westley, William A. (1953). Violence and the police, *American Journal of Sociology* 59(1): 34-41.

Westmarland, Louise (2008). Police cultures, in *The handbook of policing 2nd ed.*, ed. Tim Newburn, 253-280, London: Willan.

Wilson, James (1968). *Varieties of police behavior: The management of law and order in eight communities*, Cambridge, MA: Harvard University Press.

Worden, Robert E. (1989). Situational and attitudinal explanations of police behavior: A theoretical reappraisal and empirical assessment, *Law & Society Review* 23: 667-711.

_____ (1995). The causes of police brutality: Theory and evidence on police use of force, in *And Justice For All: Understanding and Controlling Police Abuse of Force,* ed. William A. Geller and Hans Toch, 31-60, Washington, D.C.: Police Executive Research Forum.

_____, Robin Shepard, and Stephen Mastrofski (1996). On the meaning and measurement of suspects' demeanor toward the police: A comment on demeanor and arrest, *Journal of Research in Crime and Delinquency* 33(3): 324-332.

_____ and Robin Shepard (1996). Demeanor, crime, and police behavior: A reexamination of the police services study data, *Criminology* 34: 83-105.

Yates, Donald, Vijayan Pillai, and Joel Humburg (1997). Committing to the new police-community partnerships in the United States and England, *Policing and Society* 7: 99-115.

Index